GREEN
&BLACK'S

CHOCOLATE RECIPES

The mysterious *Theobroma cacao* grows wild in the Amazon River Basin and the foothills of the Venezuelan and Colombian Andes, where it is believed the first cacao trees were found.

GREEN & BLACK'S

CHOCOLATE RECIPES

FROM THE CACAO POD TO
COOKIES, DESSERTS, AND SAVORY DISHES

Written and compiled by Caroline Jeremy
Photography by Francesca Yorke

KYLE BOOKS

"Chocolate makes otherwise normal people melt into strange states of ecstasy" *John West*

To the Maya cacao farmers
and all those cooks who have shared
their recipes over the years.

CONTENTS

FOREWORD BY JOSEPHINE FAIRLEY

When Green & Black's was launched in 1991, we cheekily declared it to be "guilt-free" chocolate. As the world's very first organic chocolate, it gave passionate chocolate-lovers a way to indulge their tastebuds without having an environmental impact – because conventionally grown cacao is still one of the most heavily sprayed food crops in the world. Because Green & Black's was organic – just beginning, then, to be a buzzword – people were intrigued enough to buy and try it. But we know that what makes someone buy any Green & Black's treat a second time – and a hundredth time – is sheer deliciousness. Quite simply, every new Green & Black's creation has to be the best of its kind that we've ever tasted. End of story.

Gradually, though, in the last decade, most of us have begun to think much more about where our food comes from. And at Green & Black's, we like to think we've helped change the world – one bar of chocolate at a time. Because we weren't just the world's first organic chocolate. In 1993, our orange-and-spice Maya Gold Chocolate became the very first product to carry the Fairtrade Mark – the shopper's guarantee that the farmers and growers who produce our cacao get a fairer price for their crops.

This was a shopping revolution. The day of Maya Gold's launch, Green & Black's had a total of eight minutes' of news coverage on primetime TV. Because Maya Gold's debut coincided with an independent campaign for fair trade, we discovered to our astonishment that thousands of Young Methodists were actually running from town to town carrying flaming torches and button-holing supermarket managers to stock this ground-breaking Fairtrade-marked product. One supermarket buyer complained to us that he'd even been getting phone calls from vicars, badgering him to stock Maya Gold because of its ethical integrity. (Nothing to do with us, though we were secretly thrilled to have that unexpected boost to our sales drive!) But that buyer still placed an order – and today, awareness of fair trade issues means most global coffee-shop empires even offer a Fairtrade-marked *cappuccino* on their menus, while shoppers can fill shopping baskets not only with fairly traded chocolate and cocoa powder, but tea, coffee, bananas, and more.

Actually, we didn't have to do anything very special to get that Fairtrade Mark: it was how we naturally did business. It was only later that we realized that we had established a blueprint for socially responsible business which many big companies are striving towards today. Green & Black's already paid a higher price than the world price – because we offered a premium for organic beans. We gave the farmers the security of long-term contracts – because we also needed that security, at a time when organic cocoa wasn't traded anywhere on the world markets and we needed to be sure of a reliable supply. Since then, though, we've been able to see the incredible impact that fair trade has on a community.

When we first started buying cacao from the Maya Indians in Belize, children left school at eleven because their parents couldn't pay for their board during the week at the high school in Punta Gorda, or even afford their essential high school books. Now, as a result of the secure income from Green & Black's, a whole generation of children from the hillside villages where our chocolate grows is being educated to the age of eighteen; some are even attending university and at least one plans to study medicine. As Cayetano Ico, the former chairman of the co-operative of cacao farmers who produce the cacao for Maya Gold once said: "when you buy a bar of Green & Black's, you're sending a child to school." Shopping ethically really does change lives and communities for the better. But we've always believed: fairly traded products also have to be as yummy – or yummier – than what else is out there. Otherwise, shoppers wouldn't buy them more than once, and then the lives of Third World farmers and growers wouldn't be transformed, after all.

People often ask how Green & Black's got its name. In fact, it was dreamed up one rainy Saturday night by me and my husband, Whole Earth Foods founder (and now Chairman of the Soil Association), Craig Sams, while searching for a name for the chocolate we planned to launch together. There was never a Mr. Green & a Mr. Black, I'm afraid: just a couple sitting in bed with a notepad and a pen, having terrific fun brainstorming. As a lifelong candy-lover, I remembered confectionery brands from my childhood, that had stayed in my mind: Callard & Bowser, Barker & Dobson. And so Green (because it was organic) & Black's (because the chocolate was such a dark brown, it was almost black) was born. If we'd stuck to some of the names we originally batted back and forth – like "Eco-Choc" or "Bio-Choc" – that very same dark chocolate would simply have gathered dust on the shelves, and very few people would have discovered its tastebud-caressing deliciousness. And somehow I don't feel I'd be writing the introduction to a cookbook devoted to it.

Our other important "first," meanwhile, was that Green & Black's was the first chocolate with 70% cocoa content available in the UK. In continental Europe, chocolate *aficionados* have long enjoyed the rich, bitter intensity of really dark chocolate. But in England, the "dark" chocolate we all grew up with actually contained as little as 30% cocoa. But since Green & Black's was launched, 70% dark chocolate has become the magic figure quoted by cookbook writers and superchefs whenever they publish a recipe that uses chocolate: quite simply, for the ultimate in chocolatiness, there's nothing better.

In the early days at Green & Black's, we printed a small recipe leaflet that featured recipes from leading chefs (at Launceston Place and The Groucho Club), alongside temptations from our (much-missed) friend Linda McCartney and others who'd generously shared their outrageous chocolate creations with us. We always dreamed, one day, of a Green & Black's cookbook, featuring the ultimate chocolate recipes – and here it is. Caroline Jeremy has done a marvelous job of writing this book, and collating (and testing) the many recipes sent to us over the years, by Green & Black's lovers, and also of persuading other leading cooks and chefs who are fans to reveal to us (and to you) their chocolate recipe secrets.

We hope you enjoy making, eating, and sharing them. Entirely guilt-free, naturally.

Josephine Fairley

INTRODUCTION

Christened *Theobroma* which means "food of the gods," cocoa is indisputably one of the most desired and valuable substances in the world. Purists would say that it is at its best used in a bar of chocolate, unadulterated by any other taste. But we think it can be just as exciting when transformed into a dessert or cake, or more unexpectedly, into a hearty stew.

Chocolate can surprise even the greatest of chefs, but it is not difficult or frightening to use. Be patient and gentle and take your time. Above all, chocolate should not be hurried. Green & Black's Dark Chocolate with 72% cocoa solids with extra cocoa butter has been created as the chocolate to cook with. The extra cocoa butter makes the chocolate very easy to work with when melting and molding. The flavor has not been compromised.

Any recipe in this book made with good-quality chocolate will taste dramatically different if made with an inferior chocolate, so choose your chocolate carefully. For most of the recipes, we have used our Dark Chocolate, which has 72% cocoa content and very little sugar. A chocolate with such a high coca content is the best to use for cooking because its intense flavor is not easily overpowered by competing flavors or other ingredients. Avoid dark chocolates that have less than 60% cocoa content and are not made with natural vanilla. Vanillin, which is an artificial flavoring, and vegetable fat, gives the chocolate a very different flavor and texture from chocolate that contains natural vanilla and cocoa butter.

Where milk chocolate is specified, try to use milk chocolate that has at least 34% cocoa content. White chocolate only contains cocoa butter from the cacao bean, not the dark solids. If white chocolate does not declare a percentage of cocoa content, it will not contain cocoa butter. It will probably also not have natural vanilla in it, which gives our chocolate its unique flavour.

An unsweetened cocoa powder is best for baking.

COOKING WITH CHOCOLATE

• Always store chocolate in a cool, dry place and do not expose to direct light. Chocolate that has been exposed to extremes in temperature or light will "bloom," or have whitish-gray streaks on it. These streaks indicate that the cocoa butter in the chocolate has changed its structure and crystallized on the surface. This does not affect the flavor though, and once melted, the chocolate will be fine to use for cooking.

• Never store chocolate near other household items or foods that have a strong scent. Chocolate absorbs odors easily and will soon taste of other flavors if stored near them. This is especially true of mint, citrus fruit, perfumes, and chemicals, so be careful when packing your shopping.

Chocoholic, n. 1. Someone whose constant craving for and delight in chocolate suggests addiction. 2. A person who eats chocolate compulsively.

• To melt chocolate, break or chop it up into even-sized pieces using your hands or a large serrated bread knife. Place it either in a heatproof bowl or double boiler and set over a saucepan of simmering water. Never allow steam or water to come into direct contact with the chocolate, and make sure the bottom of the bowl or top pan is not touching the water. This is especially important if you are melting white chocolate, which is particularly sensitive to over-heating. After two minutes, turn off the heat and leave the bowl over the saucepan of hot water while the chocolate slowly melts. Stir gently as soon as most of the chocolate has melted, and remove the bowl from the heat.

• Chocolate can also be easily melted in a bowl in a microwave oven. Cook on medium for one minute, then, depending on the quantity, in 30-second bursts. Keep checking the chocolate by prodding it with a spoon as it will keep its shape despite it having melted.

• Chocolate that has been overheated may "seize" or become very thick and lumpy and impossible to use. If this does happen, you can try whisking in a tablespoon of butter or a little vegetable oil, but you may not be able to save it if it has gone too far.

• Try to have melted chocolate at a similar temperature to the mixture you are adding it to.

• Never try to melt chocolate by adding a hot mixture to solid chocolate or vice versa, unless the recipe specifically instructs you to. The result will be grainy in texture.

• Melting chocolate with liquids is fine if specified but start melting all the required ingredients together – never add any once the chocolate has begun to melt as this may cause it to seize.

• If you need to grate chocolate, place the bar in the fridge overnight before grating and make sure your hands are cold.

• Tempering chocolate, described in detail on page 150, is only necessary if you are dipping or coating for an extremely important occasion and want to guarantee a brittle snap and gloss. Tempering is a complicated procedure, but as bars of chocolate are already tempered when you buy them, you could try this simpler version instead.

SIMPLE TEMPERING

The stable fat crystals do not melt until 94°F so, in theory, if the chocolate is never heated above 91–92°F, the temper won't be lost. The trick is to barely melt the chocolate. Into a bowl, grate the chocolate finely so it will melt quickly and evenly. Heat a thick-bottomed saucepan of water until it boils and then remove from the heat. Place the bowl of chocolate over the saucepan and stir gently, but constantly, until the chocolate has melted. For dark chocolate, the temperature should end up between 89–91°F and between 87–89°F for milk and white. It is then ready to use.

Caroline Jeremy

MAGIC

The magical ingredient in chocolate comes from a pod
that grows out of the trunk of a tree.

Lora Zarubin is a former chef and found great satisfaction running her own restaurant in Manhattan in the 1990s. For over 10 years, she has been food editor for *House & Garden*, and her extensive travels throughout Europe and Asia have made her quite an expert on partnering flavors to bring out the best in each other. This match of dark chocolate with Piment d'espelette is a perfect example – the dried, ground red chile from Spain's Basque region adds to the layers of flavor found in chocolate.

CHOCOLATE CUPCAKES
WITH PIMENT D'ESPELETTE

Preparation time: 45 minutes
Cooking time: 25 minutes
Use: Two 12-hole muffin tins, cupcake papers
Makes: 2 dozen cupcakes

CUPCAKES

5 ounces dark chocolate, minimum 70% cocoa content, coarsely chopped

2 cups all-purpose flour

2 tablespoons organic unsweetened cocoa powder

1 teaspoon baking soda

2 teaspoons Piment d'espelette

1 cup (2 sticks) unsalted butter, softened

1 cup granulated sugar

1 cup firmly packed light brown sugar

4 large eggs, at room temperature

1 cup heavy cream

1 teaspoon vanilla extract

SILKY CHOCOLATE ICING

1 cup heavy cream

1¼ cups granulated sugar

5 ounces dark chocolate, minimum 70% cocoa content, chopped

½ cup (1 stick) sweetened butter, diced

1 teaspoon pure vanilla extract

Melt the chocolate in a heatproof bowl set over a saucepan of simmering water for approximately 5 to 10 minutes. Stir occasionally until completely smooth. Remove bowl from pan.

Preheat oven to 350°F. Line two 12-cup muffin tins with cupcake papers. Set aside.

In a small bowl, sift together the flour, cocoa, baking soda, and Piment d'espelette. Set aside.

In a large bowl, on the medium speed of an electric mixer, cream the butter until smooth. Add the sugars and beat until fluffy, about 3 minutes. Add the eggs, one at a time, beating well after each addition. Add the chocolate, mixing until well incorporated. Add the dry ingredients in three parts, alternating with the cream and vanilla. With each addition, beat until the ingredients are incorporated, but do not over-beat. Using a rubber spatula, scrape down the batter in the bowl to make sure the ingredients are well blended and the batter is smooth.

HINT: The smaller you chop the chocolate, the faster it melts.

Carefully spoon the batter into the cupcake liners, filling them about three-quarters full. Bake for 20 to 25 minutes, or until a cake tester inserted in the center of the cupcake comes out clean.

Cool the cupcakes in the tins for 15 minutes. Remove from the tins and cool completely on a wire rack before icing.

Meanwhile, make the icing. In a heavy 2½ to 3-quart saucepan add the cream and sugar. With a wooden or rubber spatula stir over moderate heat until the sugar dissolves and the mixture comes to a boil. Then reduce the heat and let simmer for exactly 6 minutes. Remove from heat, add the chocolate, stir until it is melted, then add butter and stir until it is melted. Add the vanilla and stir.

Partially fill a large bowl with ice and water. Transfer the icing to a clean bowl that fits easily into the larger bowl with iced water. Place the bowl of icing in the larger bowl and stir frequently until completely cool.

When the icing begins to thicken remove it from the ice water and beat briskly with a rubber or wooden spatula until it becomes smooth and thick enough to spread – or like a very heavy mayonnaise. It should only take only a few seconds or maybe a minute or so of beating. If the icing remains too soft return it to the ice water briefly, then remove and beat again. Using a small cake spatula, spread the chocolate icing over each cup cake. Serve.

MAGIC

Launceston Place is a calm and friendly restaurant tucked away in Kensington, London. They gave Green & Black's this recipe in the early 1990s, when they first discovered the chocolate.

CHOCOLATE

BERRY TORTE

Preparation time: 25 minutes
Cooking time: 40 minutes
Use: a cake pan, 7^1/$_2$ –8 inches across, 2^1/$_2$ inches deep
Serves: 6

TORTE

^{1}/$_4$ cup all-purpose flour

5 teaspoons organic unsweetened cocoa powder

3 ounces dark chocolate,
minimum 60% cocoa content, broken into pieces

2 tablespoons unsalted butter

5 teaspoons heavy cream

4 egg whites

3 tablespoons sugar

3 large egg yolks

1^1/$_2$ cups raspberries

mixed berries and whipping cream to serve

ICING

one 3.5-ounce bar dark chocolate,
minimum 60% cocoa content, broken into pieces

^{1}/$_4$ cup (^{1}/$_2$ stick) unsalted butter

3 tablespoons heavy cream

1 teaspoon confectioners' sugar

Preheat the oven to 275°F. Butter the cake pan and lightly dust with flour to coat. Sift together the flour and cocoa and set aside.

Melt the chocolate in a heatproof bowl set over a pan of simmering water. Remove from the heat, add the butter and the cream, and stir well until the mixture is quite liquid. Remove bowl from pan.

Whisk the egg whites until stiff peaks form, add the sugar, and continue to whisk until thick and glossy. In another large bowl, beat together the egg yolks then gently fold in the flour mixture. Add the melted chocolate and mix well. Spoon a few dollops of egg white into the mixture, stir, then gently fold in the remaining egg whites. Gently pour half the mixture into the prepared cake pan, dot half the raspberries evenly over it, then pour the rest of the mixture on top of the berries.

Bake for 35 to 40 minutes, until a skewer inserted into the center of the cake comes out clean. Cool in the pan for 5 minutes and unmold onto a wire rack to cool.

To make the icing, melt the chocolate in a heatproof bowl set over a saucepan of simmering water. Remove from the heat, stir in the butter, cream, and confectioners' sugar. Immediately pour it over the cake to coat it completely, smoothing the icing using a metal spatula. Leave for 1 hour to set.

Serve with whipped cream and mixed berries.

HINT: Do not refrigerate this cake once you have iced it
as the icing will lose its shine.

Gerard Coleman and Anne Weyns are the founders of L'Artisan du Chocolat, the most elegant chocolate shop in London. This recipe, which adds coarse salt to the caramel, reflects their expertise in searching for and identifying unusual flavors that enhance good-quality chocolate.

CHOCOLATE AND
SALTED CARAMEL TART

Preparation time: 1 hour
Cooking time: 25 minutes
Use: 11-inch removable-bottomed tart pan
Serves: 12–14

PASTRY DOUGH

2$\frac{1}{2}$ cups all-purpose flour

$\frac{2}{3}$ cup confectioners' sugar

$\frac{1}{2}$ cup (1 stick) plus 1 tablespoon unsalted butter, cold

2 large egg yolks

CARAMEL

3 tablespoons corn syrup

1$\frac{1}{3}$ cups granulated sugar

$\frac{2}{3}$ cup heavy cream

1 level teaspoon coarse salt, such as kosher salt

2 tablespoons unsalted butter, diced

GANACHE

1$\frac{3}{4}$ cups heavy cream

3 tablespoons honey

12 ounces dark chocolate, minimum 60% cocoa content, chopped

$\frac{3}{4}$ cup (1$\frac{1}{2}$ sticks) unsalted butter, diced

To make the pastry dough, sift together the flour and confectioners' sugar and cut the butter into chunks. Place in the food processor and run it, adding in the egg yolks at the end, until a dough forms. Chill for 30 minutes. Roll out the dough on a lightly floured surface. Use to line the tart pan and prick the base. Chill in the refrigerator for about 30 minutes. Preheat the oven to 375°F.

Bake the pie shell blind by covering it with parchment paper, filling with dried beans, and cooking for about 15 to 20 minutes. Remove the beans and paper and continue to cook the pie shell for another 10 minutes or until it has developed a light golden color. Remove and let cool.

To make the caramel, put the syrup and sugar into a deep saucepan and cook over a medium heat. Continue to cook until the sugar dissolves and turns a golden brown color. At the same time, in a separate saucepan, bring the cream and salt to a boil. Remove the caramel from the heat and very gradually add the cream to the caramel, but be careful as the mixture can rise rapidly in the saucepan. Return to the heat and stir until smooth. Remove from the heat, gradually stir in the diced butter, then pour into the cooled pie shell.

To make the ganache, bring the cream and honey to a boil and pour it over the chopped chocolate. Mix carefully with a spatula, working from the center outwards. Once the mixture has cooled a little, gradually stir in the diced butter until smooth. Pour the ganache on top of the caramel and let it set in a cool place for about 4 to 6 hours.

HINT: Be sure to rest the pastry once made into a dough, the glutens in the pastry will relax, and prevent shrinkage on baking.

The English word "biscuit" and the Italian "*biscotti*" are both derived from the Latin "*biscoctus*" meaning "twice-cooked." Large glass jars of biscotti often grace the counters of Italian coffee shops and usually the biscotti have almonds or hazelnuts in them. They should always be cut at an angle, shaped like half-moons, and are the perfect partner for a liqueur or a fruity dessert.

MAYA-DUNKED

BISCOTTI

Preparation time: 20 minutes
Cooking time: 45 minutes
Makes: 12

1$^{1}/_{2}$ cups all-purpose flour

$^{2}/_{3}$ cup organic unsweetened cocoa powder

$^{3}/_{4}$ teaspoon baking powder

pinch of salt

1 cup granulated sugar

$^{3}/_{4}$ tablespoon ground espresso coffee

2$^{1}/_{2}$ ounces dark chocolate,
minimum 60% cocoa content, chopped

2 large eggs

1 large egg yolk

$^{3}/_{4}$ teaspoon vanilla extract

two 3.5–ounce bars Maya Gold chocolate, or other good-quality orange-flavored dark chocolate, broken into pieces

Preheat the oven to 350°F. Cover a cookie sheet with parchment paper.

Sift together the flour, cocoa, baking powder, salt, and sugar, and place into the food processor. Add the ground coffee and the dark chocolate. Pulse until chocolate is finely ground. In a bowl, whisk together the eggs and yolk, add the vanilla extract. Add to the food processor, process until a dough forms.

Lightly flour the surface and roll the dough into a log. Flour the surface of the dough ensuring it is coated on all sides. Place it on the cookie sheet. Bake the biscotti dough for 25 to 30 minutes, then remove from the oven and reduce the temperature to 300°F.

Remove the parchment paper with the biscotti on it from the cookie sheet and let cool. Use a serrated knife to cut across the biscotti at an angle to make slices about ½-inch thick. Place the slices on the cookie sheet and bake for about 30 minutes, until firm. Let cool.

Melt the chocolate in a heatproof bowl set over a saucepan of simmering water. Dip one end of each biscotti into the chocolate, place on a wire rack to set.

HINT: You can use any of your favorite types of chocolate to coat the biscotti.

A double chocolate mousse topped with raspberries. Serve this dessert at the end of a special dinner party with espresso coffee.

WHITE & DARK
CHOCOLATE MOUSSE
WITH RED BERRY COULIS

Preparation time: 20 minutes for each mousse
Chilling time: 2 hours for the dark mousse and then overnight for the white and dark mousse
Use: 7-inch springform cake pan
Serves: 8–10

DARK CHOCOLATE MOUSSE

one 3.5-ounce bar dark chocolate,
minimum 60% cocoa content, broken into pieces

$^1/_3$ cup confectioners' sugar

6 tablespoons ($^3/_4$ stick) unsalted butter, softened

3 large eggs, separated

scant $^1/_2$ cup organic unsweetened cocoa powder

pinch of salt

$^1/_2$ cup whipping cream

WHITE CHOCOLATE MOUSSE

two 3.5-ounce bars good-quality white chocolate,
broken into pieces

2 leaves gelatin or $^1/_2$-package granulated gelatin

1$^1/_4$ cups whipping cream

3 large egg yolks

1 cup confectioners' sugar

2 tablespoons water

2 tablespoons Grand Marnier

RED BERRY COULIS

1 pint strawberries or raspberries

$^1/_3$ cup confectioners' sugar

FOR DECORATING

1 pint fresh raspberries

To make the dark chocolate mousse, melt the chocolate in a heatproof bowl over a saucepan of simmering water. Add the confectioners' sugar and stir in the butter, then beat in the egg yolks and the cocoa and salt. Remove bowl from pan.

In a bowl, whisk the egg whites until stiff peaks start to form. In another bowl, whip the cream until thick, then gently fold the egg whites and the cream alternately into the chocolate mixture. Do not overmix, but ensure that the mixture is well blended.

Place the ring mold on a large, round serving plate. Pour the mousse into the mold and chill for about 2 hours before making the white chocolate mousse.

To make the white chocolate mousse, melt the white chocolate in a heatproof bowl set over a saucepan of simmering water. Dissolve the gelatin in about ¼ cup of cream that has been warmed in a saucepan.

Whisk the egg yolks and confectioners' sugar until thick and creamy and then add the Grand Marnier, the gelatin and cream mixture, and the melted chocolate. Whip the remainder of the cream until thick, and fold it into the white chocolate mixture.

Pour the white mousse on top of the dark mousse that has already set, and chill overnight.

HINT: This mousse should be refrigerated before serving, especially on a hot day,
but don't add the cocoa powder and coulis until you are ready to serve.

To make the coulis, purée the berries in a blender and then strain through a fine strainer into a bowl. Stir in the confectioners' sugar to taste.

To unmold the mousse, dip a metal spatula in boiling water, dry it, then slide it around the inside edge of the springform cake pan. Lift the ring mold off carefully and smooth the sides of the mousse with the knife.

To serve, scatter the mousse with whole raspberries. Pour some of the coulis onto the plate around the edge of the mousse and serve the remainder from a pitcher. Slice the mousse using a thin-bladed knife dipped in hot water and wiped dry.

Pam Williams is the founder of Ecole Chocolat Professional School of Chocolate Arts and spent 10 years as Master Chocolatier. This is a wonderful, milk chocolate ice cream that gets its darker color from the cocoa powder and a mellow taste from the brown sugar used instead of white sugar. Williams likes the slight grittiness that the cocoa powder brings to the texture along with the chocolate chips. The rich flavor comes from a good quality chocolate with a 60-75% cocoa content.

DARK MILK CHOCOLATE
ICE CREAM BONBONS

Preparation Time: 25 minutes
Cooking time: 25 minutes for completing the custard to refrigeration
Chilling: 4 hours or overnight
Makes: 1½ quarts or 32 bonbons

2 cups whole milk

¼ cup firmly packed dark brown sugar

7 ounces dark chocolate, minimum 70% cocoa content, finely chopped

¼ cup organic unsweetened cocoa powder

4 large egg yolks

⅔ cup granulated sugar

CHOCOLATE TO COAT

two 5.2-ounce bars baking chocolate with 72% cocoa content with extra cocoa butter for easier melting

Place the milk and brown sugar in a small pan and heat over a low heat until the sugar dissolves, stir frequently. Increase the heat to medium and heat until just before boiling, about 5 minutes. Set aside.

Melt the chocolate in a heatproof bowl set over a saucepan of simmering water. Stir occasionally. When melted, remove the bowl from the pan; add the cocoa powder and mix to incorporate the cocoa powder into the chocolate. Gradually add the milk and sugar mixture, stirring well until all the ingredients are thoroughly combined.

Now comes the hard part – you are going to make a custard. Place the egg yolks and granulated sugar in a saucepan and whip with a wire whisk until they are thick. Slowly add the chocolate mixture to the egg yolks and sugar, whisking to incorporate. Switch to a heat resistant spatula or metal spoon and constantly stir the mixture while you heat it over medium heat to almost a simmer. Right before the simmer point the custard will thicken, you will notice the light foam on the surface will have disappeared and the custard should coat the back of your spoon more visibly than before. This takes about 15 minutes. Immediately remove the custard from the heat.

Strain the custard through a fine sieve into a container and allow to cool with a piece of plastic wrap laid over

HINT: Remove ice cream from the freezer for about 5 to 10 minutes before serving – frozen tastebuds don't deliver the same flavor!

the surface so a skin does not form. Once the custard is cool refrigerate for at least 4 hours or overnight.

Place the chilled custard mixture in your ice cream maker and follow manufacturer's instructions. Churn for about 20 to 25 minutes. Add the grated chocolate once the ice cream looks semi frozen. Churn for another 2 to 3 minutes. Transfer to a freezer container, and freeze for at least another 1 hour before serving.

For bonbons: Place two cookie sheets lined with plastic wrap in the freezer. Once the churned ice cream has frozen in the freezer for a further hour, use a small 1-inch ice cream scoop to form into balls. Working quickly, scoop and place the balls on the prepared cookie sheets. Return to the freezer until solid – at least another hour. Once the balls are frozen put into a plastic freezer bag until you are ready to dip them. They can be stored for a month in a good freezer bag.

To dip: temper the cooking chocolate (see section on tempering chocolate on page 150). Once again, line two cookie sheets with plastic wrap and freeze. Work fast and in batches returning the coated ice cream balls before taking more out of the freezer. To coat, first scoop some tempered chocolate in a small ladle, add an ice cream ball, swirl around with a fork and lift up and drain by shaking gently with the fork. Place the coated ice cream ball on the chilled cookie sheet. Store in a rigid freezer container until required.

Only make this cake for celebrations. It was created the night before a photographic shoot when we realized the front cover of a recipe leaflet we had designed needed a photograph of a taller cake. The bottom layer is our "Dark Chocolate Mousse Cake" and the top is the "Taillevent Terrine" recipe (see page 157) picked up in the Eighties from the great Parisian restaurant that bears the name.

MARQUISE
AU CHOCOLAT

Preparation time: 50 minutes
Cooking time: 40 minutes
Cooling time: 2 hours
Chilling time: overnight
Use: 9-inch springform pan with high sides and removable bottom
Makes: 15 small, rich, slices

CAKE LAYER

melted butter for greasing

1 tablespoon ground almonds,
plus extra for dusting the pan

three 3.5-ounce bars dark chocolate, minimum 60% cocoa content (or two 3.5-ounce bars dark chocolate, minimum 60% cocoa content, and one 3.5-ounce bar Maya Gold or good-quality dark orange-flavored chocolate), broken into pieces

1 1/4 cups sugar

2/3 cup (1 1/4 sticks) plus 1 tablespoon unsalted butter

pinch sea salt or kosher salt

5 large eggs

MOUSSE

9 ounces dark chocolate,
minimum 60% cocoa content, broken into pieces

3/4 cup confectioners' sugar, sifted

3/4 cup (1 1/2 sticks) unsalted butter

5 large eggs, separated

2/3 cup whipping cream

cocoa powder for dusting

Preheat the oven to 350°F. Brush the pan with melted butter and dust with the ground almonds, shaking off any excess.

To make the cake, melt the chocolate, sugar, butter, and salt in a large, heatproof bowl set over a pan of simmering water, then remove bowl from the pan. Whisk the eggs with the ground almonds and fold into the chocolate mixture. Continue to fold until the mixture thickens. Pour into the cake pan and bake for 35 to 40 minutes. Let cool in the pan for about two hours before starting the mousse.

To make the mousse, melt the chocolate in a large, heatproof bowl set over a pan of simmering water. Remove from the heat and add half the confectioners' sugar, stir, then whisk in the butter. Whisk in the egg yolks, one at a time. Set the mixture aside.

Whisk the egg whites in a large bowl until stiff peaks start to form. Add the remaining confectioners' sugar and continue to whisk until glossy. Whip the cream until stiff peaks form.

Add one-third of the egg whites to the chocolate mixture and carefully fold to blend. Gently fold in the remaining whites, alternating with the whipped cream. Do not overmix, but ensure that the mixture is well blended. Pour the mousse over the cooled cake in the cake pan and refrigerate overnight.

Remove the pan from the refrigerator about 15 minutes before serving. Dip a metal spatula into boiling water, dry it, and slide it around the sides of the cake to loosen it from the pan, then remove the ring. Re-heat the metal spatula in boiling water, dry it, and gently smooth the sides of the mousse.

Place the cake, still on the pan's bottom, onto a large round serving plate. Dust generously with cocoa powder just before serving. Serve with crème fraîche or a custard sauce (see page 60).

Nigella Lawson is the UK's Kitchen Goddess. Lawson's television cooking series and books have helped give cooking some glamor. This Clementine Cake is very simple to make and is especially delicious when made with the Maya Gold Chocolate.

NIGELLA'S

CLEMENTINE CAKE

Preparation time: 15 minutes
Cooking time: 2 hours to cook the clementines, 1 hour to bake the cake
Use: 8-inch springform cake pan

4–5 clementines, skin on, weighing about 13 ounces

melted butter for greasing

6 large eggs

1 cup granulated sugar

2³/₄ cups ground almonds

1 heaped teaspoon baking powder

one 3.5-ounce bar Maya Gold Chocolate, or other good-quality, dark, orange-flavored chocolate

Put the clementines into a saucepan, cover with cold water, bring to a boil and simmer for about two hours. Drain and set aside to cool. Then cut each clementine in half and remove the seeds. Then pulp everything – skins, pith, and the fruit in a food processor.

Preheat the oven to 375°F. Butter the cake pan, dust with ground almonds, and shake out any excess.

Beat the eggs. Add the sugar, almonds, and baking powder. Mix well, add the pulped clementines, then stir together. Pour the mixture into the cake pan and bake for one hour or until a skewer inserted into the center of the cake comes out clean. Cover the cake with foil after about 40 minutes to prevent the top from burning. Remove from the oven and immediately grate the chocolate over the top of the cake while still in the pan. Let it cool completely. Remove from the pan and store in an airtight container.

HINT: This cake is best served the day after it is made. It must only be eaten once it has cooled as the texture becomes moist and the flavors of the almonds and oranges have taken hold.

Paul and Jeanne Rankin met while they were both traveling the world. Their passion for food grew while working in restaurant kitchens when funds ran out, and after training at Albert Roux's La Gavroche, they opened Roscoff in Belfast, which went on to win a Michelin star. Their latest restaurant, Cayenne, specializes in food with a hint of spice.

WHITE CHOCOLATE & HAZELNUT CHEESECAKE
WITH ORANGE CARAMEL SAUCE

Preparation time: 1 hour
Cooking time: 1½ hours
Cooling time: at least 3 hours or overnight
Use: 9-inch springform pan
Serves: 10–12

CRUST

1½ cups crumbled vanilla wafers

1 tablespoon sugar

3 tablespoons unsalted butter, melted

FILLING

³/₄ cup hazelnuts

¹/₃ cup granulated sugar

2¹/₄ pounds cream cheese

4 large eggs

1 large egg yolk

1 vanilla bean, split lengthwise,
or 1 teaspoon vanilla extract

1 tablespoon Amaretto

pinch of freshly grated nutmeg

11 ounces good-quality white chocolate,
broken into pieces (about 2 cups)

confectioners' sugar for dusting

ORANGE CARAMEL SAUCE

2¹/₄ cups orange juice

3 tablespoons sugar

1½ teaspoons arrowroot

2 tablespoons Grand Marnier

Preheat the oven to 400°F.

To make the crust, grind the wafers to a fine texture in a blender or food processor. In a bowl, combine the crushed wafers with the sugar and melted butter. Press the mixture onto the bottom of the springform pan.

To make the filling, roast the hazelnuts on a dry baking tray in the oven for 10 to 15 minutes until golden, then rub off their skins. Reduce the temperature to 300°F. Put the sugar, along with two tablespoons water in a pan and heat gently to dissolve, then boil until it is a rich caramel color. Place the hazelnuts on an oiled tray and pour the caramel syrup on top. Let harden, then break into pieces and pulse in a food processor until coarsely ground. Set aside.

Pulse the cream cheese in a food processor until smooth, then work in the eggs and egg yolk, the seeds scraped from the vanilla bean (or the vanilla extract), Amaretto, and nutmeg. Blend until smooth. Melt the white chocolate in a heatproof bowl set over a saucepan of simmering water. Remove bowl from pan. Add the melted chocolate to the cream cheese mixture and, finally, the ground hazelnuts. Pour the mixture over the crust and bake for about 1½ hours until lightly set. Switch off the oven and let it go cold and set. Remove from the oven and dust with confectioners' sugar.

To make the Orange Caramel Sauce, put the orange juice in a saucepan and boil rapidly to reduce it by one third. Put the sugar with one tablespoon water in a pan and heat gently to dissolve, then bring to a boil and boil until it is a rich caramel color. Reduce the heat, pour the juice into the sugar pan and simmer until dissolved. Blend the arrowroot with a little water to make a smooth paste, then stir into the orange caramel until the mixture has thickened. Strain through a wire mesh strainer and stir in the liqueur. Let it cool.

To serve, pour some sauce onto individual plates and place a slice of cake in the center.

MAGIC

Soufflés can be prepared up to the point of baking. Freeze the soufflé in the ramekins, then cook straight from the freezer. Preheat the oven to 400°F and place a baking tray in the oven to preheat as well. Add an extra 5 minutes to the cooking time.

MANGO, ORANGE, AND LEMON

SOUFFLÉS

Preparation time: 1 hour, 20 minutes
Cooking time: 10 minutes
Use: 8 ramekins or custard cups
Serves: 8

9 ounces canned mango slices (about 1 heaped cup) and their juice

4^1/$_2$ ounces dried mangoes (about ^{3}/$_4$ cup)

^{1}/$_3$ cup freshly squeezed orange juice

finely grated rind of 2 lemons

3 tablespoons melted butter for brushing ramekins

5 ounces dark chocolate, minimum 60% cocoa content, finely grated (about 1^1/$_2$–2 cups)

1 cup whole milk

5 tablespoons unsalted butter

3 tablespoons all-purpose flour

6 large eggs, separated

^{1}/$_2$ cup granulated sugar

Strain the mangoes, draining the juice into a saucepan. Add the dried mangoes to the juice in the saucepan. Bring to simmering point and cook until the mangoes are tender and most of the liquid has been absorbed.

Put the contents of the saucepan, the reserved canned mangoes, and the orange juice into a blender or food processor and process to a smooth purée. Stir in the lemon rind and let cool to room temperature.

Preheat the oven to 400°F.

Brush the insides of the ramekins with the melted butter, then sprinkle on the grated chocolate, turning the dishes to ensure all the sides are evenly coated with a thick covering of chocolate. Tap out any excess and set it aside for sprinkling over the finished soufflés. Place the ramekins on a baking tray to make it easier to remove them from the oven.

Heat the milk in a small saucepan. In a large saucepan melt the butter, then remove from the heat and stir in the flour. Return to a low heat and cook, stirring for a few minutes. When the roux starts to foam, gradually whisk in the milk. Cook over medium heat for a few minutes more, until thickened. Remove from the heat and let cool before whisking in the egg yolks, one at a time. Let cool completely and then stir in the mango and orange pureé.

Whisk the egg whites until soft peaks form. Gradually whisk in the sugar and continue to whisk until the meringue is firm. Stir a generous spoonful of meringue into the mango mixture to lighten it, then gently fold the mango mixture into the remaining meringue.

Fill the ramekins and bake for 8 to 10 minutes. Do not overfill the soufflés or they will tip over and collapse. Also, remember never to open the oven door; if you don't have a light in your oven, peep at them but try not to let too much air into the oven. The soufflés will rise dramatically.

Carefully remove the soufflés from the oven and sprinkle the reserved grated chocolate over the top. Using a spatula, lift the dishes onto small dessert plates and serve at once before they collapse.

TIME TO SHINE

The Toledo Cocoa Growers Association (T.C.G.A.) is a cooperative of 172 subsistence farmers. Most are Maya people, who grow cacao for us in Belize. The fairtrade contract and the premium price they can command for their organic cacao ensure that they have a stable economic future.

Beth Pilar and Ellen Sternau are How Sweet It Is – a high-end custom pastry and cake company. Their specialities are "dessert amuse bouches" (one-bite versions of classic and modern pastries, cakes, cheesecakes and meringues). However here they returned to comfort food – their coffee cake. It's chocolate swirled in vanilla cake with a crunchy topping of brown sugar and pecans with a hint of cinnamon.

CHOCOLATE SWIRL COFFEE CAKE

Preparation time: 30 minutes
Cook time: 45 minutes
Use: 9-inch square baking pan at least 3 inches deep
Serves: 10–12

10 ounces dark chocolate, minimum 70% cocoa content, chopped

3 cups all-purpose flour

1½ teaspoons baking powder

1½ teaspoons baking soda

1 teaspoon salt

½ cup (1 stick) unsalted butter

2 cups granulated sugar

3 large eggs

1 tablespoon pure vanilla extract

2 cups sour cream

1 cup pecans, toasted and chopped

½ cup dark brown sugar

½ teaspoon ground cinnamon

Preheat oven to 350°F. Grease cake pan and line the base and sides of the tin with greased parchment paper. Make sure the paper is a least 1 inch higher than the top of the pan.

Melt the chocolate in a heatproof bowl set over a saucepan of simmering water. Stir occasionally, until the chocolate is well melted; about 5–8 minutes.

Sift the flour, baking powder, baking soda, and salt into a bowl. Set aside.

In the bowl of a mixer, cream the butter and sugar until well combined. Add the eggs one at a time, and the vanilla. Add the sour cream and mix until thoroughly incorporated. Fold the sifted dry mixture into the cake mixture, one cup at a time, taking care not to over mix.

Stir one-third cake batter into melted chocolate. Pour the cake batter into prepared baking pan. Pour the chocolate mixture over and with a knife or spatula swirl the two colors together.

In a clean bowl, mix together the pecans, brown sugar and cinnamon and sprinkle evenly over the surface of the cake. Bake in the preheated oven for 45 minutes or until a cake tester comes out clean. Let cool in the cake tin for 15 minutes before lifting out onto a cake rack. Cool completely before serving.

HINT: Chop the chocolate with a serrated bread knife – this way the chocolate is chopped finer and you will also notice that the chocolate does not jump off the chopping board while cutting.

Amanda Allen has always enjoyed trying recipes from historical cookbooks and has found some intriguing combinations in medieval cooking. She adapted this recipe from Valentina Harris's book, *Regional Italian Cookery*. If you like a strong gamey flavor, you will love this dish, which was invented for the wedding of Caterina de Medici in the early sixteenth century and is typical of the flavors of the time.

TUSCAN SWEET AND SOUR
HARE STEW

Preparation time: 30 minutes
Cooking time: 2 hours
Serves: 4–6

1 large hare, portioned

5 cloves garlic, crushed

2 sprigs rosemary

5 tablespoons extra virgin olive oil

2 onions, chopped

2 carrots, chopped

1 fennel bulb, chopped

handful parsley

handful basil

3 bay leaves

6 sage leaves

1$^1/_4$ cups Chianti

2$^1/_2$ cups game stock

1 cup pine nuts

$^1/_4$ cup golden raisins

$^1/_3$ cup candied peel

1 tablespoon granulated sugar

3 cavalluci or almond cookies, ground

2 ounces dark chocolate, minimum 60% cocoa content, broken into chunks

3 tablespoons red wine vinegar

Heat half the oil in a skillet. Add the hare and brown on all sides, about 10 minutes; add the garlic and rosemary half way through. Remove from the skillet with a slotted spoon, discard the garlic and rosemary, and set the hare aside.

Heat the remaining oil in a Dutch oven. Add the onions, carrots, fennel, herbs, and the rest of the garlic and sauté for 10 minutes.

Add the hare to the vegetables and herbs, then add the wine and heat for a few minutes, stirring well. Add the game stock, bring to the boil, reduce the heat, cover and cook for 1 hour and 30 minutes.

In another saucepan, mix together the pine nuts, raisins, peel, sugar, cavalluci, chocolate, and $^1/_2$ cup water. Heat for 10 minutes over low heat, then remove from the heat and add the vinegar. Pour into the hare stew, stir, then cook for another 10 minutes.

HINT: This dish is best if left to cool overnight and then reheated the next day, as this gives the rich flavors time to infuse and develop.

Elizabeth Karmel grew up in North Carolina where she was raised on BBQ. Karmel is generally regarded as America's female grilling expert. Her two chocolate recipes in this collection demonstrate her hold on traditional sweet favorites with a touch of fire (see Ancho-chile Cherry Brownies page 165). "This pie reminds me of the rich, nutty fudge that I was addicted to in junior high school" explains Karmel. "My best friend and I traveled to Chicago and discovered Fanny May candies. The fudge was set out on a marble slab and cut to order. My favorite pieces were always the ones that had the most walnuts in them. I took the memory of that fudge and made it better with a high cocoa content chocolate and Kahlua. It's like adult fudge set in a pastry that is easy as pie to make!"

CHOCOLATE
KAHLÚA WALNUT PIE

Preparation time: 45 minutes
Cooking time: 1 hour 10 minutes
Cooling time: 1–3 hours
Use: 9-inch pie plate
Serves: 8–12

one 9-inch pie shell (see page 139 for pastry)

¾ cup walnut halves

5 ounces dark chocolate, minimum 70% cocoa content, coarsely chopped

3¹/₂ tablespoons butter, melted

²/₃ cup granulated sugar

¹/₂ cup dark corn syrup

2 large eggs, beaten

¹/₈ teaspoon salt

1 teaspoon pure vanilla extract

2 tablespoons Kahlúa

Preheat oven to 375°F.

Line the crust with parchment paper and fill with pie weights or dried beans. Bake for 20 minutes; remove the paper and weights from the crust. Continue baking until the crust is pale golden, about 5 minutes more. Transfer crust to a rack to cool slightly while preparing the filling.

Melt the chocolate in a heatproof bowl set over a saucepan of simmering water, about 5 to 8 minutes, stirring occasionally. Remove the bowl from the pan.

Reduce the oven to 350°F after pre-baking the crusts.

Evenly scatter the nuts into the pie crust. Add the butter, granulated sugar, corn syrup, eggs, salt, vanilla, and Kahlúa to the bowl of chocolate and stir until well mixed. Pour the mixture over the nuts.

Bake the pie for about 50 to 55 minutes or until cooked through and crusty on top. Let cool for about 3 hours. Serve each slice with a dollop of real whipped cream flavored with Kahlúa. Alternatively, let cool only an hour and serve warm with best quality vanilla ice cream.

HINT: Since the pie so rich, it can be stretched to feed twice as many people as a regular pie.

A former chef, Sally Schneider is a regular contributor to NPR's "The Splendid Table", a syndicated newspaper columnist and author of the best-selling cookbooks, *The Improvisational Cook* (Harper Collins) and *A New Way to Cook* (Artisan). This rich, intensely chocolate cake is the perfect dinner party dessert because it is both easy to make and dazzling. It is, in reality, a luxurious permutation of a simple brownie formula made with fabulous chocolate and baked in a round cake pan. Serve the cake with whipped cream or crème fraîche, or vanilla or pistachio ice cream.

CHOCOLATE
PISTACHIO CAKE

Preparation time: 25 minutes
Cooking time: 22–25 minutes
Use: 8-inch diameter cake pan
Serves: 8

butter and flour for coating the pan

8 ounces dark chocolate, minimum 70% cocoa content, finely chopped

6 tablespoons (³/₄ stick) unsalted butter

²/₃ cup all-purpose flour

¹/₂ teaspoon baking powder

¹/₄ teaspoon salt

2 large eggs

2 teaspoons pure vanilla extract

¹/₂ cup granulated sugar

1 cup shelled pistachios, coarsely chopped plus extra to decorate

1 or 2 teaspoons organic unsweetened cocoa powder

Position the rack in the middle of the oven. Preheat the oven to 350ºF. Rub the inside of cake pan with butter. Swirl a few teaspoons of flour around to coat completely. Invert the pan and tap out the excess.

Put the chocolate and butter in a heatproof bowl set over a saucepan of simmering water. Stir occasionally until the chocolate is melted and mixture is smooth, about 5 to 8 minutes. Remove the bowl and set aside to cool. Meanwhile, sift the flour, baking powder, and salt into a bowl; whisk well and set aside.

Combine the eggs and vanilla extract in a large bowl. Whisk until foamy. Add the sugar and whisk until light and frothy, about 1 minute. Blend in the chocolate mixture. Add the flour mixture in 2 batches, whisking to blend completely each time. Fold in the nuts.

Pour the batter into the prepared pan. Bake for 22 to 25 minutes until a skewer inserted 1 inch from the edge comes out clean. When inserted in the center, a bit of moist batter will cling to it. Do not over bake.

Cool the cake on a rack for 10 minutes, then invert onto a plate. Invert back onto the rack so the shiny side is up. Cool the cake completely before sliding it onto a serving plate. Sift the cocoa over the top and sprinkle with extra chopped pistachio nuts. Serve.

HINT: This cake keeps for up to 3 days in an airtight container. Keep in a cool place but not in the refrigerator, as this will alter the texture of the cake.

The Lighthouse Bakery in Battersea, southwest London, makes British, European, and American breads and pastries. Elizabeth Weisberg and Rachel Duffield rely on traditional methods of hand-molding, and use long fermentation to develop the full flavor of their dough. They only make Chocolate Bread on Fridays, and on Valentine's Day the bakery makes chocolate heart-shaped rolls.

LIGHTHOUSE
CHOCOLATE BREAD

Preparation: 30 minutes
Proving time: 3 hours
Cooking time: 40 minutes
Use: 1 large baking sheet
Makes: 2 small oval loaves

1 cake fresh yeast or one package dried yeast

1^1/$_2$ cups minus 2 tablespoons warm water

^{1}/$_2$ cup sugar

1 large egg yolk

2 tablespoons unsalted butter, softened

4^1/$_2$ cups unbleached white bread flour

1 tablespoon salt

^{1}/$_3$ cup organic, unsweetened cocoa powder

9 ounces dark chocolate,
minimum 60% cocoa content, roughly chopped

1 egg yolk for glazing

Combine the yeast, water, and a generous pinch of sugar in a bowl and set aside for 5 to 10 minutes until bubbly. Add the egg yolk and butter to the yeast mixture.

If using a stand mixer, place all the remaining ingredients in the bowl and mix with the paddle for 1 minute on low speed to combine. Add the yeast mixture and mix with the paddle until well blended. Switch to the dough hook and mix first on low speed and then on medium speed until the dough is smooth and elastic – this takes about 4 minutes in total. Add a little extra water if it looks too dry.

If working by hand, combine the dry ingredients in a separate bowl and mix briefly with a spoon to blend. Then add the dry ingredients to the yeast mixture in three batches, stirring well with a spoon between additions. Add the chocolate pieces last. Knead the dough on a lightly floured surface for 8 to 10 minutes until the dough is smooth and elastic. Add a little extra water if it looks too dry.

Place the dough in a lightly oiled bowl, cover with plastic wrap and let it prove for about 2 hours in a warm, draft-free area.

Turn out the dough onto a lightly floured board and punch down. Divide into two equal pieces and shape each into an oval. Place both ovals on a greased or parchment-lined baking sheet, cover with a clean damp dish cloth, and let it prove for about 1 hour, or until doubled in size.

Preheat the oven to 450°F.

Beat the egg with a fork and brush it over the surface of the loaves. Place them on the baking sheet and bake for 15 minutes. Lower the temperature to 375°F for an additional 25 minutes. Watch the loaves carefully during the last 5 minutes to avoid scorching the tops. Cool on a wire rack.

HINT: To make the heart shapes, roll the dough into long snakes about 1 inch in diameter by 15 inches long. Shape into hearts and cut into the top cleavage and inside curves of the heart shape before baking. Make sure you keep an eye on the cooking time as chocolate bread can be ruined easily if baked for too long.

Cocoa is ranked the third most-valued commodity in world food after sugar and coffee. As a result of the pressures of international markets to produce bulk chocolate, there is a wide variety of cocoa beans and, depending on the variety, where they are grown, and how they are processed, they result in many different cocoa flavors.

Cocoa beans are classed as either bulk beans or fine beans. Fine beans are derived from the two best-quality varieties, Criollo and Trinitario. Bulk beans are mainly harvested from the Forastero variety.

The fruit of the cacao tree is an oval-shaped pod about the size of a football. It can grow as long as 14 inches and weigh up to two and a quarter pounds. When ripe, the pods can be a variety of colors: red, green, orange, or purple.

The word "cacao" (pronounced *kakow*) is derived from the name for the cacao tree, *Theobroma cacao*, and is the word we use before the beans have been fermented and dried. Once dried and ready for shipping, we use the term cocoa.

This wonderful dessert was sent to us by Anne-Marie Graepel. Her mother would rustle this up during the post-war food shortages and it is a delicious chocolate dessert that is simple to make using only ingredients from your pantry. The batter can be refrigerated for up to three days.

CHOCOLATE
LAYERED CRÊPE

Preparation time: 30 minutes
Resting time: 2 hours
Cooking time: 40 minutes
Use: 8-inch heavy crêpe pan, 8- to 9-inch round ovenproof dish,
about 1–2 inches deep
Serves: 6–8

CRÊPE BATTER

1$\frac{1}{4}$ cups all-purpose white flour

pinch of salt

$\frac{1}{4}$ cup sugar

3 large eggs

2$\frac{1}{4}$ cups milk

zest of 1 orange

$\frac{1}{3}$ cup plus 1 tablespoon unsalted butter, melted

butter or oil for greasing

FILLING

1$\frac{1}{3}$ cups golden raisins or raisins

1 tablespoon Cointreau

1 tablespoon water

2 heaped tablespoons organic cocoa powder

5 heaped tablespoons superfine sugar

10$\frac{1}{2}$ ounces apricot jam (about 1 cup)

$\frac{1}{4}$ cup ($\frac{1}{2}$ stick) unsalted butter

1 cup light cream

Soak the raisins in the Cointreau and water. Sift the flour and salt into a bowl, mix in the sugar, and make a well in the center. In a bowl, whisk together the eggs, milk, and orange zest and stir in the melted butter. Pour into the well and, using a whisk, slowly incorporate the flour mixture into the liquid, whisking until smooth and velvety. Pour into a pitcher and let it rest in the refrigerator for 1 to 2 hours.

Before cooking the crêpes, whisk the batter again gently. It should have the consistency of thick cream; if it is too thick, add some milk. Rub a crêpe pan with a little butter or oil and place over medium heat. As soon as the butter begins to bubble, pour in a ladleful of batter. Swirl it evenly around the pan and pour any excess batter back into the pitcher. You will probably need to throw away your first crêpe. Once the crêpe is a nice golden-brown color on the underside, flip it over using a pastry spatula. You will need to keep oiling the pan after two or three crêpes. Pile them, unfolded, on a plate. You should end up with about 20 crêpes.

Preheat the oven to 360°F. Butter the ovenproof dish.

Before layering, first mix the cocoa and sugar in a bowl and have the raisins at hand. Lay a crêpe in the buttered dish, sprinkle with a half-tablespoon of the cocoa mixture and 2 teaspoons of the raisins, lay another crêpe on top, and continue alternating with the cocoa and raisins, and the crêpes, until the fifth crêpe. Spread every fifth crêpe with apricot jam instead of the cocoa and raisins.

When you get to the last crêpe, sprinkle the cocoa and sugar mixture over it and dot with slices of butter. Prick the crêpe pile with a fork and, just before putting it in the oven, pour the cream over the top.

Bake in the oven for 15 minutes until the top layer is nicely crisp. Serve immediately, using a sharp knife to cut into slices.

Nora Carey's passion for preserving was ignited when she worked on the Time Life *Good Cook* series of books while living in London. Nora's food career has ranged from working with Sir Terence Conran at Butler's Wharf, London to Disneyland Resort Paris. Her book, *Perfect Preserves*, is a must for any gardener who loves to cook, and is full of recipes for preserving and using preserves.

CHESTNUT AND CHOCOLATE
SOUFFLÉS

Preparation time: 2 hours including cooling time
Cooking time: 12 minutes
Use: 8 ramekins or custard cups
Serves: 8

1³/₄ cups firmly packed brown sugar

¹/₂ cup water

14 ounces prepared chestnuts peeled and cooked in water (jars rather than canned)

1 vanilla bean, split lengthwise

¹/₃ cup brandy

¹/₂ cup sugar

8 ounces dark chocolate, minimum 60% cocoa content, broken into pieces

1 cup whole milk

5 tablespoons unsalted butter

3 tablespoons all-purpose flour

6 large eggs, separated

confectioners' sugar for dusting

Heat the brown sugar with the water in a saucepan over low heat until it begins to boil, add the peeled chestnuts and the vanilla bean. Bring the mixture back to a boil and boil for about 3 minutes. Let cool for about 1 hour, then stir in the brandy. Cover with plastic wrap and set aside until needed.

Preheat the oven to 400°F. Brush the ramekins with melted butter and dust with sugar. Cut the preserved chestnuts in half and divide them between the ramekins.

To make the soufflé, place the chocolate and the milk in a small saucepan over low heat and stir until the chocolate has melted. In a large saucepan, melt the butter, stir in the flour, and cook over low heat, stirring, for about 2 minutes. When the roux starts to foam, gradually whisk in the chocolate mixture. Cook over medium heat, stirring, for 2 to 3 minutes until it has thickened. Remove from the heat and let cool. Whisk the egg yolks, one at a time, into the mixture.

In a large bowl, whisk the egg whites until soft peaks form. Gradually whisk in the remaining sugar and continue to whisk until the meringue is firm.

Stir a generous spoonful of the meringue into the chocolate mixture to lighten it, then gently fold the chocolate mixture into the remaining meringue.

Fill the ramekin dishes about three-quarters, otherwise the soufflés will tip over and collapse on baking. Bake 8 to 10 minutes. Also remember never to open the oven door; if you don't have a light in your oven, peep at them but try not to let too much air into the oven. The soufflés will rise dramatically. Dust with confectioners' sugar and serve immediately before they collapse.

HINT: If you wish to use fresh chestnuts, preheat the oven to 350°F. Score a cross on one side (the curved side) of each chestnut and place on a cookie sheet. Toast in the oven for 15 minutes, the skins will have peeled back. Allow to cool before peeling skins, not forgetting to remove the thinner inner skin too.

Lorna Wing is the queen of creative catering and first earned a name for herself doing witty canapés like mini fish and chips in dolly-sized cones made out of the *Financial Times*. This is her twist on Sachertorte that we featured in our very first recipe leaflet in 1993. It has stood the test of time and is the most decadent we have tasted. It also improves over time and is at its best after one week, stored in an airtight container.

LORNA WING'S
SACHERTORTE

Preparation time: 15 minutes
Cooking time: 1 hour
Use: 9-inch springform cake pan
Serves: 10

TORTE

melted butter for greasing

two 3.5-ounce bars dark chocolate,
minimum 60% cocoa content, broken into pieces

6 large eggs

1^1/$_2$ cups granulated sugar

1^2/$_3$ cups ground almonds

1^1/$_2$ teaspoons freshly ground coffee

6 tablespoons apricot jam

ICING

one 3.5-ounce bar dark chocolate,
minimum 60% cocoa content, broken into pieces

3 tablespoons unsalted butter

Preheat the oven to 350°F. Brush the pan with melted butter, then line it with parchment paper. Alternatively, butter the pan and dust with ground almonds to coat.

To make the torte, melt the chocolate in a heatproof bowl set over a saucepan of simmering water. Separate 5 of the eggs, then whisk the egg yolks, the whole egg, and the sugar until the mixture is thick and creamy.

In a separate bowl, whisk the egg whites until stiff peaks form.

Add the ground almonds, coffee grounds, and melted chocolate to the egg yolk mixture and stir well. Gently fold in the egg whites and pour into the prepared pan.

Bake for 1 hour, covering the cake with foil after 40 minutes to prevent the top from over browning. A skewer inserted into the center of the cake should come out clean. Release the spring-form ring but leave the cake on the bottom part of the pan to cool on a wire rack.

Melt the apricot jam over a low heat, strain, and then brush it over the cooled cake.

To make the icing, melt the chocolate in a heatproof bowl set over a saucepan of simmering water. Add the butter and stir until it has the consistency of thick pouring cream. Pour the icing evenly over the cake, smoothing it over the top and sides using the back of a metal spatula. Let it set.

HINT: Make a pattern of rings on the top and around the sides of the cake using the back of a teaspoon and then pipe "Sachertorte" in the traditional style.

This recipe comes from Elisabeth Luard, whose mouth-watering article about chocolate made it irresistible and reminds us that wild meat benefits from a sweet-sour marinade and long, gentle cooking. Agrodolce, or sweet and sour sauces, originated in Roman times, when honey, sweet wine, dried fruit, vinegar, and spices were used to mask any unpleasant flavors from the meat, which was not always very fresh, and also to counteract the effects of the preserving salt.

ITALIAN VENISON

AGRODOLCE

Preparation time: 40 minutes
Marinating time: 12 hours minimum
Cooking time: 2 hours
Serves: 6

3¹/₄ pound venison (shoulder or haunch), cubed or cut into long strips

MARINADE

1³/₄ cups red wine

3 tablespoons red wine vinegar

3 tablespoons olive oil

1 carrot, chopped

1 large onion, sliced

1 celery stalk including the head, chopped

3 cloves garlic, crushed

sprig rosemary

sprig thyme

4 sage leaves

3 bay leaves

1 teaspoon juniper berries, crushed

¹/₂ teaspoon black peppercorns, crushed

STEW

3 tablespoons olive oil

3¹/₂ ounces pancetta or bacon, diced (about ²/₃ cup)

1 medium onion, very thinly sliced

1 tablespoon all–purpose flour

1 tablespoon raisins

1 teaspoon ground cinnamon

¹/₂ teaspoon grated nutmeg

salt and pepper

1-2 tablespoons pine nuts

2-3 squares dark chocolate, minimum 60% cocoa content

Put all the marinade ingredients into a large bowl and stir well. Add the prepared venison and stir, then leave in a cool place overnight, or preferably two nights.

Remove the meat from the marinade and pat dry with paper towels. Strain the marinade and set aside.

Preheat the oven to 300°F.

Heat the oil in a Dutch oven and gently fry the pancetta until the fat runs and it browns a little. Remove and set aside. In the same oil, brown the venison, in batches, to avoid overcrowding the pan. Remove and set aside. Add the onion, season lightly, and cook until soft. Sprinkle in the flour until it absorbs some of the fat, scraping up the caramelized bits. Add the reserved marinade and the raisins, bring to a boil, and cook rapidly for 3 to 5 minutes to burn off the alcohol.

Return the pancetta and venison to the pot, bring to the boil, then add the spices, the salt, and the pepper.

Cover and cook in the oven for 1 hour and 30 minutes, until the meat is soft enough to cut with a spoon. Add a little hot water every now and then if it looks as though it is drying out.

Toss the pine nuts in a dry pan over low heat to toast.

When the meat is tender, stir in the dark chocolate until melted and the sauce is thick and shiny. Sprinkle with toasted pine nuts before serving.

TIME TO SHINE

If you like stollen you will adore this chocolate version created by Liz Usher, who had tried in vain to find a recipe for chocolate bread and decided to create one herself for our National Trust competition.

MAYA GOLD

STOLLEN

Soaking time: 12 hours
Preparation time: 30 minutes
Proving time: 30 minutes
Cooking time: 35 minutes
Use: 12 x 8-inch roasting pan
Serves: 10

3 ounces mixed dried fruit, chopped

¹/₄ cup candied peel, chopped

¹/₃ cup dark rum

zest and juice of 1 orange

one 3.5-ounce bar Maya Gold Chocolate,
or good-quality dark orange-flavored chocolate

¹/₃ cup candied cherries

DOUGH

2³/₄ cups white bread flour

¹/₄ cup organic, unsweetened cocoa powder

¹/₄ teaspoon salt

¹/₂ teaspoon grated nutmeg

1 teaspoon apple spice

2 teaspoons dried yeast

²/₃ cup milk

¹/₂ cup (1 stick) plus 1 tablespoon unsalted butter

¹/₄ cup light brown sugar

2 large eggs

COCOA MARZIPAN

1 cup ground almonds

²/₃ cup confectioners' sugar

¹/₄ cup cocoa powder

DECORATION

¹/₃ cup confectioners' sugar

¹/₄ cup cocoa powder

Mix the mixed candied fruit and candied peel in half of the rum, and stir in the orange zest and juice. Let soak overnight.

Roughly chop the chocolate into small chunks and quarter the cherries. Mix with the soaked fruits.

To make the dough, combine the flour, cocoa, salt, nutmeg, apple spice, and the yeast.

Gently melt together the milk and ⅓-cup of the butter, stir in the sugar until dissolved. Let cool. Separate one of the eggs, reserving the white. Beat the yolk with the other egg and whisk into the cooled milk mixture. Make a well in the center of the dry ingredients, add the liquid, and mix well.

Turn out and knead gently on a lightly floured board. Place in the bowl, cover with plastic wrap and leave to rise in a warm place for 30 minutes while you make the marzipan.

Line the roasting pan with parchment paper.

Preheat the oven to 375°F.

HINT: If you like a soft crust on your stollen, place a roasting pan filled with water in the bottom of the oven when baking. The steam produced will stop the crust from hardening.

To make the marzipan, mix together the ground almonds, confectioners' sugar, and cocoa with the reserved egg white. Knead lightly together in the bowl until a pliable ball forms. Roll out to an oblong about the length of the pan.

Melt together the remaining butter and rum.

Turn the dough out onto a lightly floured board. Knead a little, then roll it out into an oblong about ¼-inch thick.

Brush the dough with some melted butter and rum. Place half the fruit mixture on the top two-thirds of the dough, then fold the bottom third, two-thirds of the way up the oblong, then fold down the top third over it. Seal the edges with the rolling pin. Turn the dough clockwise so that the right-hand edge is now at the bottom, then roll it out into an oblong again. Brush again with the butter and rum and cover the top two-thirds with the remaining fruit mixture, fold, seal, and roll again as before. Do not turn it this time.

Place the marzipan in the center of the dough, fold in the two sides to meet in the center, and place, join-side down, in the lined pan. Brush the top with butter and rum and bake for 35 minutes.

As soon as you remove the stollen from the oven, brush with the remaining butter and rum mixture (which you may need to reheat slightly) and then dredge heavily with confectioners' sugar. Let cool, then sprinkle with cocoa powder for serving.

MELTING

After they have been picked, the pods are carefully cut open with a machete to reveal up to 45 beans surrounded by a gooey, white pulp. The beans and pulp are then removed by hand.

This exquisite tart is from Sue Lawrence's *Book of Baking* which is full of amazingly original recipes including Haggis Bread and an irresistible Rhubarb and White Chocolate Tart.

CHOCOLATE-CRUSTED

LEMON TART

Preparation time: 40 minutes
Chilling time: 3 hours minimum
Cooking time: 35 minutes
Use: 9-inch removable-bottomed fluted tart pan
Serves: 6

PASTRY DOUGH

1¼ cups all-purpose flour

¼ cup cocoa powder

pinch of salt

¼ cup confectioners' sugar

½ cup (1 stick) plus 1 tablespoon unsalted butter, chilled and diced

1 large egg yolk

2 tablespoons cold water

FILLING

3 ounces dark chocolate, minimum 60% cocoa content, grated (about 1 cup)

3 juicy unwaxed lemons

¾ cup sugar

4 large eggs

⅔ cup heavy cream

confectioners' sugar for sprinkling

To make the pie crust, sift together the flour, cocoa, salt, and confectioners' sugar. Rub in the cold butter using a food processor or your fingertips, until the mixture resembles fine breadcrumbs.

Mix the egg yolk with the water, and add to the mixture to make a dough. You may need a little more water. Gather the dough into a ball, wrap it in plastic wrap and chill in the refrigerator for about 1 hour.

Roll out the dough from the center and away from you, then back to the center and down towards you, using your weight to push down on it to avoid stretching it. Line the tart pan.

Prick the pie shell with a fork in several places and chill for at least 2 hours or overnight.

Preheat the oven to 400°F.

Line the pie shell with parchment paper and baking beans and bake for 15 minutes, then remove the paper and beans and bake for another 5 minutes. (Be careful not to overbake as the chocolate crust can quickly develop a bitter taste.) Remove the pan from the oven and reduce the temperature to 350°F.

While the pie crust is still hot, scatter the grated chocolate evenly over the bottom and then let cool.

To make the filling, finely grate the zest from the lemons into a mixing bowl. Squeeze and strain the lemon juice and add it to the zest along with the sugar. Whisk until the sugar has dissolved, then whisk in the eggs and the cream until the mixture is smooth.

Pour the filling into the cooled pie shell and carefully return it to the oven. Bake for 30 to 35 minutes until just set but still a bit wobbly. Remove from the oven and leave on a wire rack to cool completely before removing from the pan.

Dust with confectioners' sugar before serving.

HINT: If you love making pastry dough, try to find yourself a rolling pin with ball bearings in it! You can often pick up large, old ones at flea markets. They are the best because they are heavy, so you don't have to put as much effort into rolling.

MELTING

The pulp that cocoons the deep beet-red, pink, or white beans inside the pod is placed in wooden boxes and lined with banana leaves. They are then covered with more banana leaves and left for about five days to ferment.

The action of fermentation kills the beans and breaks down the sugars whilst other compounds and enzymes react together to produce the precursors of the first chocolate flavors.

Unfermented bulk beans are often used in cheaper chocolate blends where their poor taste can be disguised using additional processing techniques and strong flavors.

Margaret Iveson is a bit of a chocolate addict, along with most of her family and many of her friends. As far as chocolate cakes go, she declares this one is one of the most satisfying and, she also claims, indestructible. Perfect for lazy days like Sundays.

SUNDAY
CHOCOLATE CAKE

Preparation time: 30 minutes
Baking time: 25 minutes
Use: two 8-inch diameter cake pans

1¹/₂ cups all-purpose flour

¹/₄ cup organic unsweetened cocoa powder

2 teaspoons baking powder

1 teaspoon baking soda

1 teaspoon lemon juice

scant cup milk

¹/₃ cup plus 1 tablespoon unsalted butter, softened

³/₄ cup sugar

2 large eggs, beaten

¹/₂ teaspoon pure vanilla extract

SYRUP

¹/₄ cup apricot jam

2 tablespoons lemon juice

1 tablespoon kirsch

BUTTER CREAM FILLING

one 3.5-ounce bar dark chocolate,
minimum 60% cocoa content

¹/₄ cup (¹/₂ stick) unsalted butter

1 cup confectioners' sugar

1 large egg yolk

ICING

2 ounces dark chocolate,
minimum 60% cocoa content

2 tablespoons unsalted butter

1 tablespoon rum

Preheat the oven to 375°F. Butter and flour the cake pans.

Sift together the flour, cocoa, baking powder, and baking soda three times.

Stir the lemon juice into the milk to curdle it.

In a large bowl, cream together the softened butter and sugar until fluffy. Beat in some of the egg, then some of the flour mixture, then some of the milk and lemon juice. Continue in this way, beating vigorously between each addition, until the batter is fairly stiff (don't add all the milk if it seems to be getting too liquid). Finally add the vanilla extract.

Divide the batter between the pans and bake for 20 to 25 minutes, until springy to the touch. Leave the cakes in their pans for a few minutes and then turn them out to cool on to a wire rack, so that the top crust is on the bottom. Prick the bottoms gently all over.

To make the syrup, simmer the jam, lemon juice, and kirsch and pour it evenly over the cooled cakes.

For the Butter Cream Filling, melt the chocolate in a heatproof bowl set over a saucepan of simmering water. Remove bowl from pan. In a separate bowl cream together the butter and confectioners' sugar. Beat in the egg yolk, then the chocolate. Spread butter cream onto one of the cake surfaces and sandwich with the other cake.

To make the icing, melt the chocolate as above, and remove bowl from pan. Beat in the butter, then the rum and chocolate, and continue to beat until glossy. Allow to cool slightly before pouring over the top of the cake. Let it set.

MELTING

The only drink for a very hot summer's day or on a balmy night – sip and feel yourself cool down. Iced Mocha Coffee is also perfect as a dessert after a barbecue or *al fresco* lunch.

ICED

MOCHA

Preparation time: 15–20 minutes
Marinating time: 8 hours minimum, or up to 1 week
Chilling time: 2 hours
Makes: 6 tall glasses

7 ounces (about 1 cup) fresh cherries

1¼ cups brandy or port

4 cups strong, freshly ground, brewed coffee

½ cup good-quality hot chocolate powder

6 tablespoons demerara (raw) sugar

2¼ cups dark chocolate ice cream

2¼ cups vanilla ice cream

1 cup heavy cream

cocoa powder or dark chocolate for sprinkling

Marinate the cherries in the brandy or port overnight, or preferably for up to 1 week, in the refrigerator.

Make the coffee and while it is still hot stir in the hot chocolate and the sugar to taste. Remember not to make the mocha too sweet as the ice cream will be an additional sweetener.

Chill the mocha in the refrigerator until very cold. Remove the ice cream from the freezer and let soften for 10 minutes. Pour the mocha into 6 glasses, only three-quarters full, to allow enough room for 2 balls of ice cream.

Drop 3 or 4 marinated cherries into each glass and then, using an ice cream scoop, carefully drop 1 ball of vanilla ice cream into the mocha, then 1 ball of chocolate ice cream on top. Try not to disturb the ice cream too much as it will cloud the lovely dark mocha coffee. Pour 1 to 2 tablespoons of cream over the top of the ice cream and then sprinkle some cocoa or dark chocolate flakes over it. Serve immediately.

HINT: You can use leftover brewed coffee, but if it has cooled, don't reheat it. Just pour a little hot water over the hot chocolate powder before you add it to the coffee. If it is an unbearably hot day, put some ice cubes into the mocha before you add the ice cream.

Sylvia Sacco made this tiramisu for the end-of-filming party for Gilly Booth's film *One Dau Trois 123*, in which Sylvia played the leading lady. The recipe belongs to her mother, Sonia Nicastro, and lives up to its name, which means "pick-me-up." The exhausted film crew couldn't get enough of it and the recipe was immediately nabbed for this book.

SYLVIA'S

TIRAMISU

Preparation time: 25 minutes
Chilling time: minimum 2 hours or overnight
Use: 9-inch serving dish, about 3 inches deep
Serves: 6

7 ounces Savoiardi cookies or ladyfingers

1$^1/_2$ cups espresso or strong brewed coffee, cold

$^1/_4$ cup Grand Marnier or Marsala

4 large eggs, separated

$^1/_2$ cup granulated sugar

14 ounces mascarpone cheese

pinch of salt

2 tablespoons organic unsweetened cocoa powder

Working in batches of 4, dip half of the cookies into the coffee then use to line the base of the serving dish. Drizzle cookies with half of the liqueur.

Whisk together the egg yolks and sugar until thick and creamy, add the mascarpone cheese, and stir well until smooth and thick. Whisk the egg whites until stiff peaks form and add a pinch of salt. Gently fold the egg whites into the mascarpone cheese and egg mixture.

Spoon half the mixture over the cookies in the bottom of the dish. Repeat soaking of cookies in coffee, then place over mascarpone mixture. Place the remaining cookies on top of the mixture. Drizzle with the rest of the liqueur. Cover with the remaining mascarpone cheese and egg mixture. Sift the cocoa powder evenly over the top.

Cover with plastic wrap and chill for at least 2 hours, or preferably overnight.

HINT: It is important for the coffee to be cold. Otherwise the cookies will soak in too much liquid and may cause the tiramisu to be too runny.

Deryl Rennie made this loaf cake so that she could enjoy her two favorite flavors at once. The pieces of chocolate sink into the batter so that they embed themselves at the bottom of the loaf while the lemon gives the cake a refreshing edge.

LEMON DRIZZLE

WITH SUNKEN DARK CHOCOLATE CHUNKS

Preparation time: 15 minutes
Cooking time: 40 minutes
Use: 5 x 7-inch loaf pan
Serves: 10

BATTER

$^1/_2$ cup (1 stick) plus 1 tablespoon unsalted butter

$^1/_2$ cup granulated sugar

2 large eggs

1 cup self-rising flour

1 teaspoon baking powder

grated rind of 1 large lemon

1 tablespoon milk

3 ounces dark chocolate,
minimum 60% cocoa content, chopped

LEMON DRIZZLE

$^1/_4$ cup firmly packed light brown sugar

juice of 1 lemon

Preheat the oven to 350°F. Line the loaf pan with parchment paper.

Whisk the butter, sugar, eggs, flour, baking powder, and lemon rind together for about 2 minutes. Whisk in the milk to make a soft dropping consistency. Stir in the chocolate.

Spoon the mixture into the prepared pan, smooth the surface, and bake for 40 minutes or until the center of the cake springs back when gently pressed. Remove from the oven.

Stir the light brown sugar into the lemon juice and pour it over the hot cake in its pan. Make a few holes with a fine skewer if the lemon icing remains on the surface.

Remove the cake from its pan and place on a wire rack, leaving it in its paper (if using) to cool completely.

HINT: If you use grated chocolate, it will give the cake a speckly appearance.

Lori Longbotham is the author of *Luscious Chocolate Desserts* (Chronicle) and a former food editor for *Gourmet*. The combination of caramel and chocolate is quite brilliant. To make a caramel sauce is not as scary as it may first seem. Watch the syrup carefully, swirling it occasionally until the syrup is a dark caramel color. Do not allow the caramel to become too dark as the sauce will become bitter; if the caramel is too light, the sauce will be too sweet…but it's easy for the eye to see the difference.

CHOCOLATE
CARAMEL SAUCE

Preparation time: 10 minutes
Cooking time: 20 minutes
Makes: 2 cups

4 ounces dark chocolate,
minimum 60% cocoa content, coarsely chopped

1 cup warm water

pinch of fine grain salt

2 cups granulated sugar

2 tablespoons light corn syrup

1 cup heavy cream

Melt the chocolate with ¼ cup of the water and the salt in a heatproof bowl set over a saucepan of simmering water. Stir occasionally until thoroughly melted, about 5 to 8 minutes. Remove bowl from the pan and set aside.

Put the sugar, remaining ¾ cup of the water and corn syrup in a large heavy pan. Set the pan over a medium heat, stirring until the sugar dissolves. Be careful not to splash the sugar up the sides of the pan. Increase the heat to high and bring to a boil, washing down the sides of the pan with a damp pastry brush if you see any sugar crystals forming. Boil without stirring, until the caramel turns a dark golden brown, continuing to wash down the sides of the pan if necessary. Remove from heat.

Meanwhile, heat the cream in a small pan until hot. Remove the pan from the heat. Being careful to avoid the spatters, stir in the warm cream about 2 tablespoons at a time into the caramel. Return the caramel to a low heat and cook, whisking until the sauce is smooth. Remove the pan from the heat, add the chocolate mixture, and whisk until smooth.

Use immediately or let cool to room temperature, transfer to a glass jar, and refrigerate until ready to serve.

HINT: The sauce can be stored in the refrigerator for up to 2 months,
simply reheat what you need adding a little water or cream if necessary to thin slightly.

SAUCES

TOFFEE BAR

one 3.5-ounce bar Toffee Chocolate, broken into pieces

4 tablespoons milk

Melt the chocolate with the milk in a small saucepan over a very low heat until the chocolate and toffee pieces are melted and combined with the milk. Let it cool for a few minutes and then pour over cake or use as a sauce for ice cream.

SIMPLE CHOCOLATE

one 3.5-ounce bar dark chocolate, minimum 60% cocoa content, chopped

$^1/_2$ cup heavy or whipping cream

1 tablespoon unsalted butter

Melt the chocolate along with the cream in a heatproof bowl set over a saucepan of simmering water, stirring frequently. Once the chocolate has melted, add the butter and stir until it has melted. Serve warm.

ALASTAIR LITTLE'S CHOCOLATE FUDGE

$^1/_2$ cup heavy cream

$^2/_3$ cup granulated sugar

2 tablespoons unsalted butter

$^1/_3$ cup corn syrup

$^1/_3$ cup whole milk

$^1/_2$ teaspoon vanilla extract

one 3.5-ounce bar dark chocolate, minimum 60% cocoa content, broken into pieces

Put all the ingredients, except the chocolate, in a heavy saucepan over medium heat, stirring constantly until the mixture is a pale caramel color. This will take about 10 to 15 minutes after coming to a slow boil. Remove from the heat and beat in the chocolate pieces. Stir in 3 tablepoons of cold water. If the mixture is still too thick, continue adding water, a spoonful at a time, until you achieve a good pouring consistency. Serve immediately or keep warm in a water bath until needed.

CUSTARD

1 vanilla bean

1$^1/_4$ cups whole milk

2 large egg yolks (3 if you want a very thick sauce)

1 heaped tablespoon sugar

Split the vanilla bean lengthwise, scrape out the seeds, and put both bean and seeds in a saucepan along with the milk. Bring to a boil, remove from the heat and let infuse for 15 minutes. Beat the egg yolks and sugar until thick and creamy. Remove the vanilla bean from the milk and pour into the egg mixture. Pour it back into the saucepan and heat gently, stirring constantly with a rubber spatula, until the sauce thickens, do not boil. The custard will coat the back of a spoon. Remove the custard from the heat and strain into a bowl. Serve warm or chilled.

CUSTARD WITH MINT

Make the recipe as above but substitute the vanilla bean with a handful of chopped mint. Add Crème de Menthe to taste once the custard has cooled a little. Another name for this sauce is Mint Crème Anglaise.

Pastry chef and cookbook author, Emily Luchetti honed her dessert-making skills at the celebrated Stars restaurant. Her books include *Stars Desserts*, and *Four Star Desserts*. This chocolate chip ice cream is adapted from Luchetti's book, *A Passion for Desserts* (Chronicle). It's a simple all cream, no custard-style ice cream – four ingredients for a super creamy textured ice cream.

CHOCOLATE CHIP
ICE CREAM

Preparation time: 10 minutes
Chilling: 1 hour + churning
Use: ice cream machine
Makes: 1 quart

$^1/_2$ vanilla bean, split lengthwise
and seeds removed

4 cups whipping cream

$^1/_2$ cup granulated sugar

5 ounces dark chocolate,
minimum 72% cocoa content, finely chopped

Place a freezer container in the freezer to chill ready for when you need to transfer the freshly churned ice cream.

Place the vanilla bean and seeds into a medium saucepan with the cream and sugar. Warm the mixture over a medium heat, stirring occasionally, until the sugar dissolves, about 5 minutes. Once you see bubbles around the edge of the pan, remove from the heat.

Transfer the cream mixture to a bowl and set over another bowl filled with iced water. Stir the cream occasionally until cooled; remove the bowl from the water bath. Remove and discard the vanilla bean. Cover the cream with plastic and chill for at least 1 hour.

Transfer the cream to the pre-chilled ice cream canister and churn according to manufacturers instructions; about 20 minutes until semi frozen. Add the chopped chocolate and fold in with one or two turns of the machine. Spoon the ice cream into the prepared chilled container. Smooth the surface and return to the freezer. Freeze for at least 1 hour before serving.

If made several days ahead, you may need to remove the ice cream from the freezer about 10 minutes before required to soften it a touch.

LICKING THE BOWL

With the only high school far away in Punta Gorda, many cacao farmers' children have to board with families near the school. Without the extra income generated from Fairtrade organically grown cacao, their parents would not be able to afford the cost of their accommodation and the weekly bus fare.

LICKING THE BOWL

At the end of a kids' party, serve fruit splits in cones. Have the cones ready dipped and decorated with chocolate. Let the children choose which dried fruit to put into the cones, then the fruit and ice cream combos they prefer.

FRUIT SPLIT

SURPRISE

Preparation time: 15 minutes

chocolate and vanilla ice cream

milk chocolate bars, for dipping the cones

quality wafer ice cream cones

chopped nuts or chocolate or candy strands for coating the chocolate-dipped cones

dried fruits such as raisins, golden raisins, blueberries or cherries to put in cones

YOUR CHOICE OF:

melon, cut into tall slices

bananas, cut in half

pineapple, cut into long tall chunks

dragon fruit, sliced into quarters, skin on

kiwi fruit, sliced lengthwise

drinking chocolate powder, for decorating

Remove the ice cream from the freezer and let it soften for 10 minutes. Melt the chocolate in a heatproof bowl set over a saucepan of simmering water. Remove the bowl from the pan.

Dip the tops of the cones in the melted chocolate and then into the chopped nuts. Stand the cones upright in medium to tall glasses to dry.

Put some dried fruit in the bottoms of the cones. Then place softened ice cream on one side of the cone and slices of fruit in the other side of the cone so that they stick out at the top. Wedge more ice cream into the cone to help hold the fruit up, then sprinkle with the chocolate powder.

HINT: Look out for freeze-dried strawberries and raspberries to crush and sprinkle over the finished cones.

Bea Hovell is seven years old and she loves baking. She usually makes her Thumbprint Cookies with jam as a filling, but has found that our chocolate spread seems to be another perfect partner for them. Remember chocolate spread has hazelnuts in it so do be careful who you give them to!

BEA'S

THUMBPRINT COOKIES

Preparation time: 20 minutes
Resting time: 1 hour
Cooking time: 10–12 minutes
Makes: 18–24

³/₄ cup (1¹/₂ sticks) unsalted butter, softened

³/₄ cup granulated sugar

1 large egg

1 cup self-rising flour

1¹/₃ cups all-purpose flour

7 ounces chocolate hazelnut spread (about 1 cup)

Line 2 cookie sheets with parchment paper.

Cream the butter and sugar until light and fluffy using an electric beater. Add the egg and beat well. Stir in the two flours and mix to a dough. Let it rest for 1 hour.

Preheat the oven to 350°F.

Measure a scant tablespoon of dough. Roll the dough between your palms to form 1-inch balls. Place on the cookie sheet and flatten slightly. Press your thumb into the middle of the dough to make a hole. Continue with the remaining dough. Place the cookies at least 2 inches apart on the cookie sheets. Using a teaspoon, fill each hole with the chocolate spread.

Bake for 10 to 12 minutes or until the cookies are just golden. Cool on a wire rack.

HINT: Place a dishtowel under the bowl to prevent it from slipping while you are beating, and put four little dots of butter on the baking tray before you line it with parchment paper to stop the paper from shifting.

After fermentation, the beans are spread out on mats to dry in the sun and raked over intermittently. In sunny weather, drying the beans usually takes about a week.

Susan Spungen, a trained pastry chef was the founding food editor and Editorial Director for Food at Martha Stewart Living Omnimedia from its launch in 1991 until 2003. Peanut butter and chocolate are childhood favorites.

PEANUT BUTTER
GANACHE BARS

Preparation time: 20 minutes
Cook time: 25 minutes
Use: 9 x 13 inch non-stick baking pan
Makes: 32

FOR THE COOKIE LAYER

1¹/₄ cups all-purpose flour

¹/₂ teaspoon baking soda

¹/₄ teaspoon salt (preferably flaky sea salt, pulverized)

¹/₂ cup (1 stick) unsalted butter

1 cup natural peanut butter (smooth)

¹/₂ teaspoon pure vanilla extract

¹/₂ cup firmly packed dark brown sugar

¹/₂ cup granulated sugar

1 large egg

³/₄ cup Rice Krispies

FOR THE GANACHE LAYER

One 5.2-ounce bar dark chocolate, minimum 70% cocoa content, coarsely chopped

8 ounces sour cream

2 tablespoons unsalted butter, at room temperature, diced

¹/₄ cup light corn syrup

¹/₂ teaspoon vanilla extract

Preheat oven to 325°F.

In a bowl, sieve together flour, baking soda, and salt.

In an electric mixer fitted with the paddle attachment, cream the butter and the peanut butter until well combined. Add the vanilla and sugars. Mix well and scrape the sides with a rubber spatula. Add half the dry mixture and mix until just incorporated. Add the egg and mix well. Add the remaining dry mixture and Rice Krispies and mix until dough just comes together.

Press into the base of a non-stick 9x13 inch baking pan. Bake for 20–23 minutes, until barely golden on top, rotating halfway through. Remove from the oven and let cool completely on a wire rack.

Meanwhile, make the ganache. Melt the chocolate in a heatproof bowl set over a saucepan of simmering water. Stir occasionally until smooth. Remove the bowl from the pan, set aside and let cool slightly. Meanwhile, warm the sour cream, in its container with the lid removed, in the microwave or in a bowl of warm water, until just warm.

Stir the butter into the chocolate, then the sour cream, corn syrup, and vanilla, until well combined. It should be silky smooth. Let cool, stirring occasionally, until firm enough to spread. When the cookie is completely cool, spread the ganache evenly over the entire surface in soft swirls or stripes. Set aside to allow the ganache to firm, cut into 32 rectangles and serve.

Penny Parker hosts heavenly teas and has many recipes that people are always asking for, which she is very happy to pass along. These Chocolate Oat Bars contain muscovado sugar, which gives them a rich mellow flavor.

CHOCOLATE
OAT BARS

Preparation time: 10 minutes
Baking time: 20 minutes
Use: 7 x 11-inch baking tray or roasting pan
Makes: 20

1¹/₂ cups (3 sticks) unsalted butter

3 tablespoons corn syrup

³/₄ cup firmly packed soft brown sugar

³/₄ cup muscovado sugar (if unavailable, use soft brown sugar)

1¹/₂ cups good-quality oats (oat flakes)

3 cups processed oats (rolled or porridge oats)

6 tablespoons organic unsweetened cocoa powder

Preheat the oven to 275°F.

Melt the butter, syrup, and both sugars in a large saucepan, stir until the sugars dissolve. Do not let them bubble. Mix in the oats and the cocoa until thoroughly combined.

Pour the contents of the saucepan into the baking pan and, using a fork, press the mixture into the baking pan until even. Bake for 18 to 20 minutes. The oat bars need to cook to the center but you do not want them to bubble, otherwise they will be too toffee-like. They should stay moist.

Remove from the oven and let cool for about 10 minutes. Slice when warm. Let cool completely before removing from the tray.

HINT: These oat bars are delicious with two tablespoons of dried shredded coconut, or a handful of golden raisins added with the oats. Equally tasty is one tablespoon of sesame seeds, but you will also need a handful of extra oats because the seeds will make the oat bars oily.

Fun to make and adored by children, you only have to look at the ingredients to see why. These balls of chocolate caramel are a recipe from jewelry designer, Valerie Black, and one which reminds her of her childhood in Argentina. Adjust the cocoa to taste and cover the Brigadeiros in anything from confectioners' sugar to chocolate sprinkles. Adults with a sweet tooth love them with a dusting of cocoa.

BRIGADEIROS

Preparation time: 15 minutes
Cooking time: 30 minutes
Cooling time: 2 hours

one 14-ounce can of condensed milk

2–3 tablespoons organic unsweetened cocoa powder

unsalted butter for greasing

confectioners' sugar, chocolate sprinkles, or other covering

To make the caramel, pour the condensed milk into a saucepan, add cocoa to taste, and place over medium heat. Stir the caramel regularly and with care because it will be very hot. Once it begins to thicken, stir continuously until the caramel separates as you drag the spoon through it.

This will take about 30 minutes. Remove from the heat and set aside to cool for about 2 hours.

Sift the confectioners' sugar into a bowl. Once the mixture has cooled, rub some butter on your hands and, taking a tablespoon of mixture at a time, roll it into balls between your palms, then drop each one into the powdered sugar or chocolate sprinkles, moving it from hand to hand to dust off any excess.

Arrange on a decorative platter and serve.

HINT: The condensed milk can also be made into a caramel without the addition of cocoa powder. In Argentina it is known as Dulce de leche. Pour it on vanilla ice cream or use to make banana and cream pie.

Rose Levy Beranbaum is an internationally known food expert, and has been a featured presenter in the highly regarded Melbourne Food & Wine Festival and Oxford Food Symposium. Baking is her specialty. All her books are baking "bibles", all with respectable awards and accolades. These chocolate sugar cookies are Rose's favorite. They are intensely chocolaty and buttery yet exceptionally light. The chocolate butter cream topping is silky smooth under its crown of crunchy toasted walnuts.

CHOCOLATE COOKIES
WITH CHOCOLATE BUTTER CREAM

Preparation time: 30 minutes
Cooking time: 7 to 10 minutes per batch (at least 2 batches)
Use: 2 large cookie sheets
Makes: 34 cookies

SUGAR COOKIES

½ cup and ⅔ cup (4¼ ounces) lightly toasted walnuts, divided

¼ cup (¾ ounce) sifted organic unsweetened cocoa powder

⅓ cup (about 1⅓ ounces) confectioners' sugar

⅓ cup (about 2⅓ ounces) granulated sugar

⅔ cup (1 stick 2 tablespoons/5 ounces) unsalted butter, softened

¾ cup (3¾ ounces) bleached all purpose flour

CHOCOLATE WALNUT BUTTER CREAM

3 ounces dark chocolate, preferably 70% cocoa content, coarsely chopped

3 tablespoons (1½ ounces) unsalted butter, softened

½ teaspoon corn syrup

½ teaspoon pure vanilla extract

Position 2 oven racks in the upper and lower thirds of the oven. Preheat the oven to 325°F. Line the cookie sheets with baking parchment.

Grate ½ cup of the nuts until fine. Roughly chop the remainder to medium coarse.

Put the grated nuts in a medium size bowl and whisk together with the cocoa and sugars. Put the softened butter in a large bowl with the sugar mixture and beat with an electric mixer until light and fluffy. Add the flour in 2 batches, mixing on a low speed with the electric mixer.

Measure scant tablespoons of dough. Roll the dough between your palms to form 1-inch balls. Place them 2 inches apart on the cookie sheets. Use a flat-bottomed glass tumbler, dipped in granulated sugar, to flatten the dough to about 1½ inches in diameter.

Bake the cookies for 20 to 25 minutes or until they are firm enough to lift from the sheets, but still soft when pressed lightly on the top. Cool the cookies on the sheets for 2 minutes. Transfer them to racks to cool.

While the cookies are baking, prepare the walnut butter cream. Melt the chocolate in a heatproof bowl set over a saucepan of hot water, stir occasionally. Remove the bowl from the heat and gradually stir in the butter until melted. Stir in the corn syrup and vanilla. Stand at room temperature for about 1 hour or until thick enough to spread.

Use a small metal spatula to spread the butter cream on the cookies and sprinkle with the chopped nuts on top. Allow the topping to set overnight at room temperature or refrigerate for 30 minutes.

LICKING THE BOWL

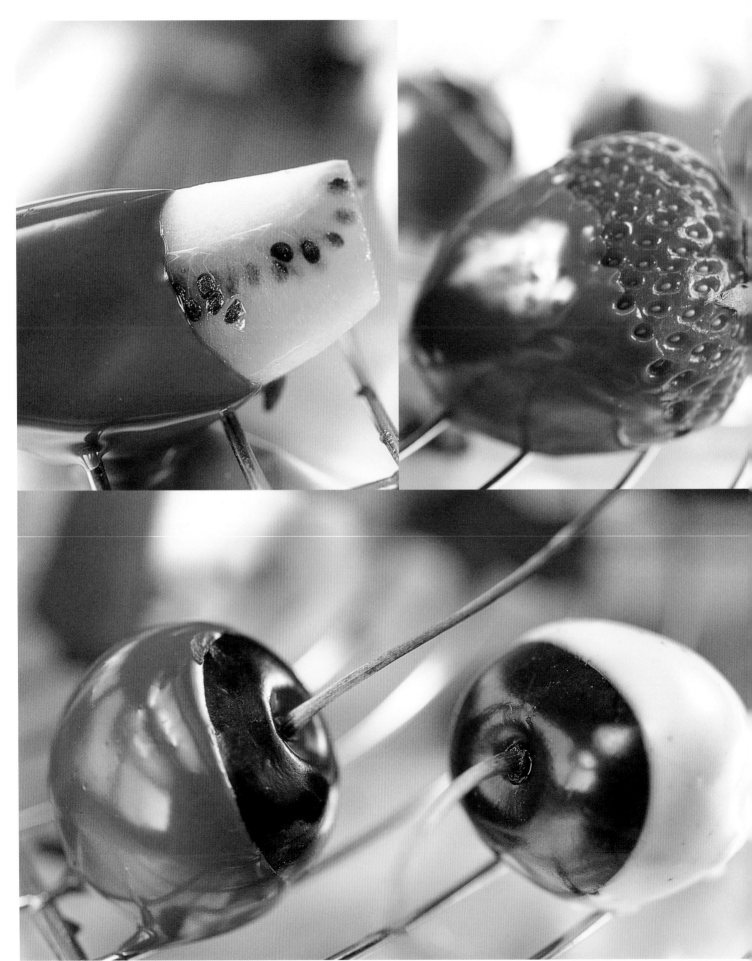

Haley Foxen is the goddaughter of our founder, Josephine Fairley. Haley's mother was the chairman of the Soil Association and, along with Jo and Craig Sams, was a driving force in the campaign for the return to farming methods that work in harmony with nature and that produce food with real taste. Haley gave us this recipe when Green & Black's was first launched.

CHOCOLATE
DIPPED FRUIT

Preparation time: 30 minutes
Use: wire rack, or toothpicks and a block of styrofoam, or two halves of a watermelon to support the dipped fruit
Makes: about 100 pieces

one 3.5-ounce bar milk chocolate,
preferably 34% cocoa content, broken into pieces

one 3.5-ounce bar good-quality white chocolate,
broken into pieces

one 3.5-ounce bar Maya Gold, or a good-quality,
dark, orange-flavored chocolate, broken into pieces

12 strawberries, stems in place

2 ripe kiwi fruit, sliced

12 cherries, stalks in place

1 pineapple, cut into triangular pieces

2 bananas, sliced at an angle

2 mangoes, sliced

1 carton Cape gooseberries (also known as physallis)

2 dragon fruit (a Vietnamese red-skinned cactus
fruit), sliced into quarters, skin on

Melt the three chocolates separately in heatproof bowls each sitting over its own saucepan of simmering water. Take extra care with the white chocolate. Let cool for about 5 minutes before dipping the fruit.

You can use toothpicks to skewer the prepared fruit, dipping the pieces so that each one is half-covered with chocolate, then stick them in the styrofoam or watermelon to set. Alternatively, hold the fruit with your fingers, dip them into the chocolate and let them set on a wire rack. Continue until all the chocolate is used up.

Once dipped, do not put the fruit in the fridge otherwise the chocolate will lose its shine.

HINT: You can also freeze the prepared fruit before dunking it in the chocolate
and then return it to the freezer on a tray lined with waxed paper
for a sweltering, summer's day treat.

Muffins are very simple to make. You can simplify the recipe even more by making them with the all-in-one method. Place all the ingredients in a bowl, mix for 2 minutes with an electric handmixer. Sprinkle the top of unbaked muffins with raw brown sugar for a crunchy finish.

BANANA, CHERRY, AND WHITE CHOCOLATE

MUFFINS

Preparation time: 10 minutes
Cooking time: 20 minutes
Use: paper muffin cups and a 10-cup muffin pan
Makes: 10 large muffins

1 cup all-purpose flour

$1/2$ tablespoon baking powder

$1/4$ teaspoon salt

1 large egg

3 tablespoons caster sugar

$1/2$ cup whole milk

$1/4$ cup ($1/2$ stick) unsalted butter, melted

2 ounces dried cherries, chopped (about $1/4$ cup)

2 ounces white chocolate, chopped (about $1/3$ cup)

1 small ripe banana, mashed

Preheat the oven to 400°F. Line the muffin pan with paper cups.

Sift together the flour, baking powder, and salt. In a separate bowl whisk together the egg, sugar, milk, and melted butter. Mix the dry ingredients into the wet ingredients. Don't try to blend them too evenly – they should remain a little lumpy. Add the cherries, white chocolate, and mashed banana and stir, but again, do not overmix.

Spoon into the paper muffin cups, filling each approximately two-thirds full.

Bake for 20 minutes until well risen and golden. Leave to cool for 10 minutes before removing from pan.

HINT: The muffin batter should not be evenly blended otherwise the muffins will have too smooth a texture and will be more like cupcakes.

Chocolate pancakes make a good change from the usual breakfast pancakes. Add raisins or dried blueberries. Serve warm with slices of banana and maple syrup, or chocolate sauce and ice cream for a dessert.

CHOCOLATE

DROP SCONES

Preparation time: 15 minutes
Cooking time: 20 minutes
Use: heavy frying pan and spatula
Makes: 18–20

³/₄ cup self-rising flour

1 teaspoon baking powder

3 tablespoons granulated sugar

¹/₄ cup organic unsweetened cocoa powder

1 large egg

²/₃ cup whole milk

¹/₃ cup (³/₄ stick) unsalted butter

grated zest of 1 orange or
teaspoon grated fresh ginger (optional)

Sift the flour, baking powder, sugar, and cocoa into a large bowl. Make a well in the center and drop in the egg. Beat the egg, gradually drawing in the flour. Slowly add the milk a little at a time, mixing the ingredients to form a smooth batter the consistency of thick pouring cream. Keep your actions gentle otherwise the drop scones will be tough.

Stir in one of the optional flavorings if you like.

Melt the butter in the frying pan over low heat and then pour it into a heat-resistant measuring cup and keep it by the stove.

Test the frying pan's temperature by cooking one drop scone first. Pour a tablespoon or so of the batter onto the hot, greased pan. Let it cook until a few bubbles appear on the surface and burst, then flip it, and let it cook on the other side for 1 minute.

If the pan seems hot enough, then continue to cook the remaining drop scones in the same way, cooking three at a time and leaving lots of space between them so they don't run together. Add more melted butter to the pan between batches and make sure the entire surface of the pan is greased before pouring in the next batch.

Add more melted butter to the pan between batches and ensure it covers the surface fully before cooking the next batch.

Serve immediately with butter, chocolate spread, maple syrup, honey or chocolate sauce and bananas.

HINT: To reheat, wrap in layers of aluminum foil and place in a warm oven for a few minutes.

CREATE A STIR

The dried beans must contain less than seven to eight percent moisture,
to prevent mold growth during storage.

These will surprise you and only get better as you devour them and the heat of the chiles takes hold. Chile is one of the oldest partners for chocolate and this is a great way to eat them, and a wonderfully unusual treat. Helen Garmston, one of the runners-up in our *Country Living* magazine recipe competition, first made these muffins as a dessert for a Mexican buffet supper. They are equally good for breakfast or brunch.

MEXICAN MOLE
MUFFINS

Preparation time: 15 minutes
Baking time: 20 minutes
Use: 12-cup muffin pan, 24 paper muffin cups
Makes: 12 muffins

one 3.5-ounce bar milk chocolate, preferably 34% cocoa content

$1/2$ ounce or more fresh red chiles (thumb- or finger-length chiles are likely to be medium hot), about 2 tablepoons

$1^1/_2$ cups all-purpose flour

$1/_4$ cup organic unsweetened cocoa powder

1 teaspoon baking powder

$1/_2$ teaspoon salt

$1/_2$ cup granulated sugar

2 medium eggs

$1/_2$ cup sunflower oil

1 cup whole milk

1 teaspoon pure vanilla extract

Preheat the oven to 400°F. Line a 12-cup muffin pan with double paper muffin cups.

Coarsely grate the milk chocolate. Finely dice the red chiles, discarding the seeds and membrane, being careful not to touch the flesh of the chiles. It is best to use rubber gloves.

Sift the flour, cocoa, baking powder, and salt into a bowl, and stir in the sugar, grated chocolate, and diced chile. Make a well in the center.

In another bowl, beat the eggs and sunflower oil until foamy, then gradually beat in the milk and vanilla extract. Pour the dry ingredients into the well and stir until just combined. Don't be tempted to overmix, otherwise they will not have the rough texture of a traditional muffin.

Spoon the mixture into the paper cups, filling each two-thirds full. Bake for approximately 20 minutes, until the muffins are well-risen and springy.

Let the muffins cool in the pan for a few minutes and serve them warm, or turn them onto a wire rack to cool completely.

HINT: If you do touch the flesh of the chiles with your bare hands, be extra careful not to touch your eyes.

The beets in this cake give it a moist, velvety texture and just a hint of a purple color. The flavor is distinctively of beets and rather earthy, with a smooth mellow taste from the dark chocolate. Most cakes with vegetables in them were first made because of a surplus of home-grown vegetables.

CHOCOLATE

BEET CAKE

Preparation time: 30 minutes
Cooking time: 50 minutes
Use: 7-inch round cake pan
Makes: 8 slices

1 cup organic unsweetened cocoa powder

1³/₄ cups self-rising flour

1 cup light brown sugar

one 3.5-ounce bar dark chocolate,
minimum 60% cocoa content, broken into pieces

¹/₂ cup (1 stick) unsalted butter, diced

9 ounces cooked beets (about 1¹/₂ cups)

3 large eggs

FOR SERVING

confectioners' sugar for dusting

crème fraîche

Preheat the oven to 350°F.

Butter and flour the cake pan, and shake out any excess flour.

Sift together the cocoa and the self-rising flour, then mix in the sugar. Melt the chocolate and butter in a heatproof bowl set over a pan of simmering water for about 5 to 8 minutes. Stir occasionally. Remove bowl from pan.

Purée the beets in a food processor, whisk the eggs, then stir them into the puréed beets. Add the beet and the chocolate mixtures to the dry ingredients and mix together thoroughly.

Pour the mixture into the cake pan. Bake for 50 minutes or until a skewer inserted into the center comes out clean. Remove from the oven and let the cake remain in its pan for 10 minutes before turning it out onto a wire rack to cool. Serve dusted with confectioners' sugar and some crème fraîche.

HINT: If liked, you can dice golden and red beets, toss in sunflower oil and honey and roast until tender and caramelized. Then purée for the recipe.

Delicate hands are needed for this hedonistic dessert sent to us by Phillip Harris-Jones, who grows his own chiles. Late one night towards the end of a dinner party, he served thinly sliced chiles that had been marinating in vodka with a bar of Green & Black's Dark Chocolate; one thing led to another and his next dinner-party guests enjoyed these unforgettable chocolates.

VODKA CHILE

CHOCOLATES

Marinating time: 12 hours
Preparation time: 30 minutes
Use: pastry bag and small nozzle
Makes: 12 chile chocolates

6 green chile peppers, stalks on

6 red chile peppers, stalks on

1¹/₂ cups vodka

one 3.5-ounce bar good-quality white chocolate or dark chocolate, minimum 60% cocoa content, to fill the chiles

black pepper, freshly ground

confectioners' sugar and black pepper, for serving

FOR DIPPING

one 3.5-ounce bar dark chocolate, minimum 60% cocoa content

Wash the chiles, then cut a small slit in the side of each one so you can remove the inner membrane and all the seeds, so they are ready to be filled. Marinate the prepared chiles in the vodka for at least 12 hours before you prepare the filling.

To make the filling, melt the white or dark chocolate in a heatproof bowl set over a saucepan of simmering water. Remove from the heat and mix in a shot of vodka and some freshly ground pepper. Fill the chiles using a pastry bag fitted with a small nozzle, or, if you don't have one, use a coffee spoon and a chopstick instead. Store the chiles in a container in the freezer until needed.

Sift confectioners' sugar over a serving plate. Grind some black pepper over the sugar.

To dip the chiles, melt the dark chocolate in a heatproof bowl set over a saucepan of simmering water. Pour the melted chocolate into a glass and dip the chiles so that they are three-quarters coated in chocolate. Place them directly onto the serving plate to set before serving.

HINT: It is possible to blanch the de-seeded chiles to soften their flavor or boil them for two minutes to remove most of their heat.

Once dried, the beans are hard and shrunken, having transformed from a white, purple, or pink color, depending on the variety, to a medium or dark brown.

The chocolate flavors are now in place, although they are not yet fully developed. The beans are ready to be shipped to the factory.

This deep, dark cake was sent to us by Viv Pearson, who was given this recipe by a friend. It is her antidote to very sweet chocolate cake and has the most sumptuous flavor. It is great served with cream or vanilla ice cream.

RICH STOUT

CAKE

Preparation time: 35 minutes
Cooking time: 1-1^1/$_4$ hours
Use: 9-inch-deep springform cake pan

1 cup (2 sticks) unsalted butter, softened

1^3/$_4$ cups firmly packed soft dark brown sugar

4 large eggs, beaten

1^2/$_3$ cups all-purpose flour

^{1}/$_2$ teaspoon baking powder

2 teaspoons baking soda

1 cup organic unsweetened cocoa powder

1^3/$_4$ cups Guinness or another stout
(let the head settle before using)

5 ounces dark chocolate,
minimum 60% cocoa content, grated
(about 1^1/$_2$ cups)

Preheat the oven to 350°F.

Butter and line the cake pan with parchment paper. Alternatively, butter the pan and dust it with flour to coat, shaking out any excess.

In a large bowl, cream together the butter and sugar until light. Gradually add the beaten eggs beating well between each addition. In another bowl, sift together the flour, cocoa, baking powder, and baking soda.

Add some of the flour to the cake batter, stir to combine, then add some stout and stir. Continue alternating with the flour and stout until all are used up and the batter is thoroughly mixed. Fold in the grated chocolate. The consistency will be quite soft.

Spoon into the pan and bake for 1 hour to 1 hour 15 minutes until a skewer inserted into the center of the cake comes out clean. Cover the cake with foil if browning too quickly.

Remove from the oven and let stand for 10 minutes before turning out onto a wire rack to cool.

HINT: Allow the head on the Guinness to settle before mixing in the cocoa.

The stew can be served with simple croutons. Dice 2 thick slices of sourdough bread into ½-inch thick cubes. Place in a baking pan with 2 tablespoons oil, 2 tablespoons melted butter, and plenty of sea salt flakes and freshly ground black pepper. Toss to mix. Bake for 15 to 20 minutes in a medium hot oven.

SWEDISH

CHOCOLATE COFFEE LAMB

Preparation time: 30 minutes
Cooking time: 1 hour
Serves: 4–6
Use: large Dutch oven

¹/₃ cup flour

¹/₂ teaspoon mustard powder

pinch of sea salt or kosher salt

freshly ground black pepper

2¹/₄ pounds very lean lamb (fillet or leg), cut into 1¹/₄-inch cubes

¹/₃ cup (³/₄ stick) unsalted butter

1 tablespoon olive oil

3 garlic cloves, crushed

1 large onion, sliced

12 shallots, peeled and finely chopped

1 tablespoon Kahlúa (or other coffee liqueur)

1 cup strong brewed coffee

4 cups good-quality lamb stock

2 ounces dark chocolate, minimum 60% cocoa content, broken into pieces

FOR GARNISHING

1 tablespoon crème fraîche or sour cream

handful chopped fresh parsley

Preheat the oven to 425°F.

Season the flour with the mustard powder, salt, and pepper. Toss the lamb in the seasoned flour and coat well. Rub together 2 tablespoons of butter and the remaining seasoned flour and set aside.

Heat the oil and remaining butter in the Dutch oven, add the garlic, onion, and shallots, and sauté for 5 minutes until soft and golden. Remove from the pan with a slotted spoon and set aside.

In the same pan, sear the flour-coated lamb in batches until browned on all sides. Add a little extra oil if necessary. Remove and set aside. Do not wash out the frying pan!

Add the Kahlúa and the coffee to the sticky brown residue in the pot and, over medium heat, stir together for about 4 minutes, scraping up all the bits from the bottom of the pan, to form a glossy smooth sauce; the sauce should be reduced by half. Add the lamb stock and the flour and butter mixture, continuing to stir. Bring to a boil. Return the onion mixture and meat to the pot. Cover.

Transfer pot to the oven for 15 minutes, then reduce

HINT: Pour boiling water over the shallots and leave for 10 minutes to loosen their skins before peeling.

the temperature to 325°F for another 45 minutes or until the lamb is tender. Insert a knife into the center of a chunk – the lamb should just slide off.

Once tender, remove the lamb from the oven and stir in the pieces of chocolate, ensuring it is completely blended throughout the stew.

Garnish with a swirl of crème fraîche or sour cream, and a sprinkling of fresh chopped parsley.

CREATE A STIR

A keen organic vegetable gardener, cook, and chocolate lover, Lindsey Barrow was one of the runners-up in our *Country Living* recipe competition. She devised this recipe "after being inundated with zucchinis from her organic garden." Lindsey often bakes this loaf for charity cake sales and, because of the unusual combination of ingredients, it always sells out.

CHOCOLATE
ZUCCHINI BREAD

Preparation time: 20 minutes
Cooking time: 55 minutes
Use: 2-pound loaf pan
Makes: 8–10 slices

CAKE

6 ounces dark chocolate,
minimum 60% cocoa content, broken into pieces

8 ounces zucchini (about one 8-inch zucchini)

1 1/2 cups all-purpose flour

1 teaspoon baking powder

1 teaspoon baking soda

1 teaspoon ground cinnamon

1/2 cup granulated sugar

3/4 cup sunflower oil

2 large eggs

FROSTING

4 tablespoons (1/2 stick) unsalted butter, softened

3 cups confectioners' sugar

1/2 cup organic unsweetened cocoa powder

water or milk

Preheat the oven to 350°F.

Brush the pan with a little oil and line the bottom with parchment paper.

Melt the chocolate in a heatproof bowl set over a saucepan of simmering water. Stir until smooth and keep warm.

Finely grate the zucchini and drain on paper towels.

Sift the flour, baking powder, baking soda, and cinnamon into a large bowl and mix in the sugar and grated zucchini.

In another bowl, beat together the oil and eggs. Pour into the flour mixture, stir, then stir in the melted chocolate.

Pour the batter into the prepared loaf pan and bake for 55 to 65 minutes, or until the loaf is well risen and a skewer inserted into the center comes out clean.

The freshly baked loaf is very fragile so let it cool in the pan for at least 15 minutes or until lukewarm, before turning it out carefully onto a wire rack to cool completely.

To make the frosting, cream the butter until light and fluffy. Sift together the confectioners' sugar and the cocoa powder, then beat into the creamed butter with enough water or milk to make a frosting that is easy to spread.

HINT: The loaf freezes well. Do not put the frosting on. Either freeze the loaf whole or ready sliced. Wrap first in plastic wrap then foil. Place in resealable plastic bag and freeze for up to 4 weeks.

Marian Ash created this quintessentially South American dish when she was reading *Like Water for Chocolate* by Laura Esquivel and then had a chat with a friend about the magical effect of chocolate on savory food. She began experimenting and came up with this recipe, which she suggests serving with corn tortillas and an avocado salad.

CHICKEN
MOLE

Preparation time: 20 minutes
Cooking time: $1^1/_2$ hours
Use: large Dutch oven
Serves: 4

2 garlic cloves

2 large onions

2 smoked, dried Jalapeño chile peppers,
soaked and chopped, soaking water reserved,
or 2 teaspoons of smoked sweet paprika

8 chicken pieces on the bone

2 tablespoons olive oil

one $14^1/_2$-ounce can chopped tomatoes

one 15-ounce can red kidney beans, drained and rinsed

$2^1/_2$ ounces dark chocolate,
minimum 60% cocoa content, broken into pieces

salt

Preheat the oven to 300°F.

Crush the garlic cloves and slice the onions.

Remove the seeds and chop the soaked chile peppers, and reserve the soaking water (at least 2 cups).

In a large Dutch oven, heat a little olive oil and sear the chicken pieces in it for about 10 minutes until browned, turning occasionally.

Remove and set aside. Add the garlic and onions to pan juices and sauté for 5 minutes until golden, add the tomatoes and the red kidney beans, the chopped chiles, their soaking juice, and two-thirds of the chocolate.

Bring to a boil, then return the chicken to the pot. Cover the pot and transfer to the oven and cook for at least 1 hour and 30 minutes.

Skim the surface to remove the fat from the chicken if necessary.

Taste, and adjust the seasoning with salt if necessary.

Add the rest of the dark chocolate to taste.

The sauce will be a rich, thick, velvety brown with a gloss all of its own.

HINT: Omit the chicken and double the quantity of beans for a vegetarian mole.

CREATE A STIR

Zanne Early Stewart joined *Gourmet* in 1972 and, as the executive food editor, Stewart led eleven talented chefs for nearly thirty years in developing and testing recipes in every issue of the magazine. In her new capacity as the magazine's media food editor, Stewart is developing content for Gourmet's video, television and website programming.

"For years I've added unsweetened cocoa powder to my chile con carne to deepen the flavors, rather along the lines of a good mole poblano sauce," explains Stewart. "Recently I realized that the small amount of sugar in dark chocolate helps balance the heat of the chiles as well. If the chile pureé is exceptionally spicy and I'm going to be serving the chile to kids as well as adults, I serve it on cooked macaroni with grated Cheddar cheese and sour cream to further tame the spice. My New England grandmother always referred to chile on macaroni as chile mac," laughs Stewart!

CHILE CON CARNE

Preparation time: 45 minutes
Cook time: 1 hour and 30 minutes
Serves: 8

2 dried ancho chiles

4 dried New Mexico or guajillo chiles

¹/₄ cup olive oil

1 large white or yellow onion, finely chopped

4 large garlic cloves, minced

1 large red bell pepper, core and seeds removed and finely chopped

1¹/₂ pounds ground chuck

1¹/₂ teaspoons ground cumin

1 teaspoon salt

¹/₂ teaspoon ground allspice

1 ounce dark chocolate, minimum 70% cocoa content, chopped

one 28-ounce can plum tomatoes, chopped (reserve juice)

Stem and seed the chiles (reserve seeds) then put in a medium pan with just enough water to cover. Bring to the boil, reduce the heat to a simmer, and cook for 10 minutes then let cool. Transfer chiles with a slotted spoon to blender, add 1 cup of the cooking liquid, and blend until very smooth. Reserve.

In a 6-quart pot, heat the oil over a medium heat. Stir in the onion and cook for 5 minutes until translucent. Add the garlic and bell pepper and cook, stirring, until bell pepper is tender, about 3 minutes. Add ground chuck and cook over moderate heat, stirring to break up lumps, just until meat is no longer pink, then stir in the cumin, allspice, and salt until well combined. Stir in the chocolate and continue until melted. Finally add the tomatoes and juice and reserved chile purée mixture. Bring to the boil, reduce the heat to medium and then to low and simmer, partially covered, for 1 hour and 30 minutes, stirring occasionally.

Serve the chile with the reserved chile seeds on the side, for those who like to have a more spicy hot chile con carne.

This recipe must be made by hand to get the right texture. Roger Slater has a large airy kitchen so he proves his bread in a preheated oven before turning the oven on again to bake it. He suggests toasting the bread and eating it on its own or with a seafood appetizer such as smoked salmon.

CHOCOLATE, CHILE, & LIME

BREAD

Preparation time: 40 minutes
Rising time: 35 minutes
Cooking time: 20–25 minutes
Use: 2-pound loaf pan

³/₄ ounces dried yeast

2 tablespoons brown sugar

about 1³/₄ cups warm water

about 3¹/₂ cups white bread or all-purpose flour

1 teaspoon salt

4¹/₂ ounces dark chocolate,
minimum 60% cocoa content, chopped

1 lime, plus the juice from ¹/₂ lime

1 dried red chile, seeded and finely chopped

¹/₄ cup olive oil

Mix together the yeast, sugar, and half the warm water to activate the yeast. Set aside in a warm place for about 15 minutes.

Sift the flour and salt into a mixing bowl, add the chopped chocolate, and the juice from the half-lime. Grate the peel of the whole lime and add the zest to the bowl. Thinly slice the lime, peel and all. Add half the sliced lime to the bowl and discard the rest. Add the chopped dried chile and the olive oil to the bowl, and mix roughly.

Once the yeast has frothed up, add it to the mixture and mix thoroughly by hand.

As the liquid is absorbed, add another ¹/₄ cup of the warm water and continue to mix. When a dough ball starts to form, use your judgement to add as much of the remaining warm water as needed. The dough should be moist but not wet. If the dough becomes too wet, sprinkle in some extra flour to absorb the excess moisture. Continue to work the dough for 15 minutes.

Place the dough on a floured baking tray. Cover with a clean damp dishcloth and leave in a warm place for at least 20 minutes to rise.

Preheat the oven to 350°F.

Lightly oil the loaf pan with olive oil and put the dough in it, pressing down and shaping, not too firmly, then turn off the oven and place the pan in the warmed oven to stand for another 15 minutes.

Then turn the oven back on again, this time to 425°F, and bake for 20 minutes.

After 20 minutes, turn the bread out of the pan and tap the bottom with a wooden spoon – it should sound hollow. If it does, place the loaf on a wire rack to cool; if it doesn't, return to the oven (without the pan) for another 5 minutes.

HINT: For dough to rise, it needs moisture and warmth and no drafts.
If the air temperature is too low, the yeast will be slow to react; too high and it will die.

One Christmas, Margaret Ruhl created this recipe as a surprise for her husband who is a connoisseur of chocolate-coated ginger. It tastes and looks fantastic with spikes of ginger rising up out of the icing and is an absolute must for any ginger and chocolate fiend.

CHOCOLATE

GINGER CAKE

Preparation time: 15 minutes
Cooking time: 1 hour
Use: 7- or 8-inch round cake pan

CAKE

$^2/_3$ cup granulated sugar

$^2/_3$ cup (1$^1/_4$ sticks) unsalted butter

3 large eggs

3 tablespoons of syrup from a jar of preserved ginger

1 cup self-rising flour

$^1/_3$ cup organic unsweetened cocoa powder

3$^1/_2$ ounces preserved stem ginger, finely chopped (about $^1/_3$ cup)

ICING

3$^1/_2$ ounces crystallized ginger (about $^1/_2$ cup)

one 3.5-ounce bar dark chocolate, minimum 60% cocoa content, broken into pieces

To make the cake, preheat the oven to 350°F. Line the bottom of the cake pan with parchment paper. Alternatively, butter the pan and dust with flour to coat, tipping out any excess flour.

Beat the sugar and butter until light and fluffy. Add the eggs, one at a time, beating well after each addition, then add the preserved ginger syrup, and lightly beat again. Sift the flour and cocoa, fold them into the mixture, then fold in the finely chopped preserved ginger.

Pour into the cake pan and bake for 1 hour or until a skewer inserted into the center comes out clean. Remove from the oven and leave in the pan for 10 minutes before turning out onto a wire rack, leaving the paper on. Let cool before making the icing.

To make the icing, finely chop the ginger. Melt the chocolate in a heatproof bowl set over a saucepan of simmering water. Add the ginger and stir well. Remove bowl from pan. Once the cake has cooled, pour the icing over the cake using a metal spatula or pastry spatula to spread it.

HINT: This cake is just as delicious with melted Maya Gold Chocolate poured over it.

TREASURES

Traces of caffeine and theobromine were discovered in 2002 in the remains of a brew found in cooking pots in northern Belize. The pots came from a Maya burial site *c.*600 B.C. and showed that chocolate was used for food 1,000 years earlier than previously thought and that it was the Maya, not the Aztecs, who were the first to make a drink from it.

Martine Hilton's mother grew up on the plantations of Sumatra and Java surrounded by cacao pods. Her father, who had trained as a chemist, devised a method of roasting the beans and then hand-grinding them to make bars of rich, fatty chocolate. This is a family recipe based upon ingredients that were available to her grandparents such as fresh coconut, cans of condensed milk, and her grandmother's favorite, hot ginger. Martine says it was often served when the ladies changed from sarongs into sweltering European dress after lunch to receive visitors. She has adapted this recipe and serves these squares at Christmas with Javanese coffee.

JAVANESE
GINGER SQUARES

Preparation time: 15 minutes
Chilling time: overnight
Use: 7 x 11-inch shallow baking pan
Makes: about 25

four 3.5-ounce bars dark chocolate, minimum 60% cocoa content, broken into pieces

1/2 cup (1 stick) unsalted butter

one 14-ounce can condensed milk

9 ounces crystallized ginger (about 2–2 1/2 cups)

9 ounces gingersnaps, crushed (about 2 1/2 cups)

3 ounces flaked coconut (about 1 cup)

Line the base and sides of the baking pan with waxed paper. Melt the chocolate in a heatproof bowl set over a saucepan of simmering water. Stir in the butter and condensed milk until smooth. Remove bowl from pan.

Finely chop the ginger into small pieces and set about one quarter aside. Stir the remaining ginger into the chocolate with the gingersnaps and the flaked coconut.

Spoon the mixture into the prepared pan spreading with a small metal spatula. Level the surface. Dot the surface with the reserved pieces of ginger.

Chill overnight in the pan. Lift out the set chocolate mixture, and cut into small squares with a thin-bladed knife.

Store in an airtight container, separating the layers with waxed paper.

HINT: Flaked coconut can be found in food stores and specialty food stores.

Florentines are another of those tempting treats that one eyes in pâtisserie windows, never imagining they could be within reach of the home cook. They are, in fact, not nearly as complicated as they look.

FLORENTINES

Preparation time: 20 minutes
Cooking time: 10–12 minutes
Cooling and decorating time: 25 minutes
Use: 2³/₄-inch cookie cutter, 2 cookie sheets, preferably non-stick, or silicon mats
Makes: about 24

4 tablespoons (¹/₂ stick) unsalted butter

¹/₂ cup heavy cream

¹/₂ cup granulated sugar

¹/₄ cup dried cherries, cut into quarters

1 cup blanched almonds, finely chopped

¹/₂ cup slivered almonds

³/₄ cup candied orange peel, finely chopped

¹/₃ cup all-purpose flour, sieved

9 ounces dark chocolate,
minimum 60% cocoa content, broken into pieces

Preheat the oven to 350°F. Line the cookie sheets with silicon mats or wax paper if not non-stick.

Heat the butter with the cream and sugar over a low heat, stirring until the sugar dissolves. Bring to the boil and remove from the heat. Stir in the cherries, almonds, and the candied peel. Gradually mix in the flour.

Drop teaspoonfuls of the mixture onto the cookie sheets, spaced 2 inches apart. Flatten with a fork dipped in cold water.

Bake for 5 to 6 minutes, remove from the oven, and shape the warm cookies into perfect circles by placing the cookie cutter over each one, and pushing excess cookie into the circle. Return to the oven and bake for another 5 to 6 minutes, until lightly browned at the edges. Let cookies set for a few minutes on the cookie sheets, then use a metal spatula to transfer them to a wire rack to cool.

Melt the chocolate in a heatproof bowl set over a saucepan of simmering water. Spread the smooth undersides of the florentines with chocolate using a metal spatula. When it is on the point of setting, create wavy lines across the chocolate by dragging a serrated knife from side to side across the chocolate. Let them set. Serve.

HINT: This recipe is also delicious using milk, white, or Maya Gold Chocolate.

This recipe was sent to us by Lorna Dowell, another of our National Trust chocolate competition finalists. Lorna was inspired to experiment after a delicious tea at the National Trust site at Dapdune Wharf, England, where she ate soft-baked chocolate chip cookies.

CHOCOLATE BRAZIL
SOFT-BAKED COOKIES

Preparation time: 15 minutes
Cooking time: 20 minutes
Use: 2¹/₂-inch cookie cutter, cookie sheet
Makes: 20

6 tablespoons (³/₄ stick) unsalted butter

¹/₄ cup granulated sugar

1 large egg, beaten

1¹/₃ cups whole wheat flour

1 cup bran

¹/₂ teaspoon salt

1¹/₂ teaspoons baking powder

¹/₂ teaspoon vanilla extract

1–2 tablespoons milk

3 ounces dark chocolate,
minimum 60% cocoa content, roughly chopped

3 ounces milk chocolate,
preferably 34% cocoa content, roughly chopped

2 ounces brazil nuts, chopped (about ¹/₂ cup)

Preheat the oven to 350°F. Line 2 cookie sheets with parchment paper.

Beat the butter and sugar in a bowl until light and fluffy. Beat in the egg. Sift the flour, salt, and baking powder once, returning the bran to the sifted flour, then fold it into the mixture. The bran gives a distinctive flavor and texture to the cookies. Beat well, adding the vanilla extract and enough milk to make a pliable dough. Mix it with your hands, adding the milk in stages until the dough is fairly soft, but not sticky. Add the chopped chocolate, and nuts, and distribute evenly through the dough. Roll out onto a lightly floured board to a thickness of about ¼ inch. Press out the cookies using the cookie cutter and place them on the greased cookie sheet, leaving plenty of room in between cookies.

Bake in the center of the oven for about 20 minutes until just golden around the edge but still soft. Leave the cookies to cool on the cookie sheet for a few minutes before transferring to a wire rack to cool completely.

HINT: All flour should be sifted before you use it. Sifting flour is important, not just to remove any little foreign bodies that may be in the flour, but also to aerate it.

TREASURES

Jeffrey Alford and Naomi Duguid are award winning cookbook authors. Their book, *Home Baking*, (Artisan) is a beautiful collection of journeys with food, as are all their cookbooks. Alford and Duguid have definitely lived it and cooked it!

Bread and chocolate is a classic combo in France. These long rolls are like mini-baguettes dotted with dark chocolate, wonderful bread with just the right amount of chocolate.

CHOCOLATE
BREAD BATONS

Preparation time: 2 hours
To prove: 13 to 33 hours
Use: 2 cookie sheets
Cooking time: 20 minutes
Makes: 24 long rolls

POOLISH

1 cup lukewarm water

⅛ teaspoon dried yeast

1 cup all-purpose flour

DOUGH

3 cups lukewarm water

1 teaspoon dried yeast

poolish (above)

2 cups pastry or cake flour (or substitute another 1½ cups all-purpose flour)

About 4½ to 6 cups all-purpose flour, plus extra for surfaces

4 teaspoons salt

10 ounces dark chocolate, minimum 72% cocoa content

Make the poolish 1 or 2 days before you wish to bake. Mix the water, yeast, and flour into a smooth batter and set aside covered in plastic wrap to ferment for 8 to 24 hours.

Place the 3 cups water in a large bowl, sprinkle on the yeast, and stir to dissolve it. Add the poolish and stir it in, then add the pastry flour and 1 cup of the all-purpose flour and stir to make a wet batter. Sprinkle on salt and stir in, then continue to add all-purpose flour, stirring to incorporate it, until a wet dough forms. Generously flour a work surface and turn the dough out onto it. Knead, incorporating flour as necessary to prevent sticking, trying to work toward a fairly soft dough rather than a stiff one. Knead for 5 minutes or more until you have a smooth soft elastic dough.

Place dough in a clean bowl and cover with plastic wrap. Set aside on your countertop to rise for 4 hours, or if more convenient, for as long as 8 hours or overnight, in a cool place.

When ready to proceed, turn the dough out onto a lightly floured surface and cut it into two equal pieces. Set aside for a few minutes while you lightly butter (or line with parchment paper) two small (12- by-9-inch) or one regular (18- by-12-inch) cookie sheets. Use a large knife or cleaver to slice the chocolate crosswise into very thin slices or shards, then cut the slices crosswise in half and set aside.

Set one piece of dough aside while you work with the other. Flatten the dough into a rectangle 8 or 9 inches wide and about 20 inches long. Sprinkle half the chocolate pieces over the dough. Roll up loosely, pulling a little on each side of the dough to stretch it wider as you roll; you will have a roll that is about 18 inches long. Flatten it with lightly floured palms to a rectangle 5 inches wide. Don't worry if a little of the chocolate is showing or pushing out of the dough.

Use a sharp knife or a dough scraper to cut the dough crosswise into twelve pieces each 1½-inches wide and 5 inches long. One at a time, pick up a piece at both ends and give it a twist while stretching it lengthwise a little, then place it on a prepared baking sheet.

Repeat for the remaining pieces, laying them side-by-side in two rows, leaving a ½-inch space between rolls. Set aside, covered, while you repeat with the second half of the dough to make another 12 rolls. Cover all rolls with plastic wrap and let rise for 1 hour before baking.

Meanwhile place a rack in the middle or lower middle of your oven and preheat the oven to 450°F. If using two baking sheets that will not fit side by side in your oven, place a second rack above the first.

Bake for 5 minutes, spritzing the rolls generously with water three times, then lower the heat to 425°F and bake for another 15 minutes. If baking on two racks, switch baking sheets around after 10 minutes. The rolls should be lightly golden when baked and they will have baked together, creating a soft place along the side of the buns where they touch. Transfer to a rack to cool. The rolls keep well for 2 days, though they rarely last that long!

HINT: You can also, once the rolls have cooled to room temperature, wrap them in two layers of foil or plastic and freeze them. To defrost, leave out overnight, still wrapped.

Roger Moore sent in this recipe with a note saying "My late mother-in-law was an accomplished cook, whose cakes and puddings were irresistible to potential sons-in-law. The origins of her recipes lay in a motley collection of old, well-thumbed cookery books, though most had been adapted using the personal touch, as they became family traditions. The Chocolate Apple Cake has always been my favorite and seems to improve over time, if any is left over for tomorrow!"

MY MOTHER-IN-LAW'S

CHOCOLATE APPLE CAKE

Preparation time: 30 minutes
Cooking time: 50–55 minutes
Use: 8^1/$_2$-inch round cake pan
Serves: 8

CAKE

2 cups self-rising flour

1 teaspoon baking powder

1^1/$_4$ cups (2^1/$_2$ sticks) unsalted butter

^{3}/$_4$ cup granulated sugar

3 large eggs, beaten

about ^{1}/$_4$ cup strong brewed coffee

1 cup hazelnuts, toasted and finely chopped

2 ounces dark chocolate,
minimum 60% cocoa content, coarsely grated

FILLING

1^1/$_2$ pounds tart cooking apples,
peeled, cored and chopped

grated rind and juice of 1 lemon

1^1/$_2$ tablespoons rhubarb jam or fruit compôte

ICING

two 3.5-ounce bars dark chocolate,
minimum 60% cocoa content, broken into pieces

1 teaspoon strong brewed coffee

two tablespoons unsalted butter

2 drops pure vanilla extract

Preheat the oven to 350°F. Butter and flour the cake pan. Sieve the flour and baking powder. Set aside.

Beat the butter and sugar together until light and creamy. Gradually add eggs beating well between each addition. Fold the flour mixture in 2 batches, and enough coffee to make a soft mix. Fold ¾ cup hazelnuts into the batter, along with the coarsely grated chocolate.

Pour the batter into the cake pan. Bake for 50 to 55 minutes until well risen and it pulls away from the pan. Let the cake cool a little in the pan, before turning out to cool completely on a wire rack.

Meanwhile, prepare the filling. Put the apples in a saucepan with the grated lemon, and jam. Cover and cook over low heat, stirring occasionally, for 10 minutes until the apple pieces are soft, but not mushy. Cool completely.

Carefully cut it in half horizontally using a serrated knife, and fill with the apple mixture.

To make the icing, melt the chocolate with the coffee in a heatproof bowl over a saucepan of simmering water. Remove bowl from the pan and stir in the butter and vanilla extract. Let cool a little before pouring over the cake, allowing the icing to run gently over the sides. Decorate with the remaining hazelnuts.

HINT: This cake can be made with almost any nuts, especially pine nuts or almonds, which do not have to be grilled.

Once they arrive at the chocolate factory, the beans are pitted and cleaned. A brief, intense blast of heat is fired at them to loosen the shells from the nibs that nestle inside. Crushers, sieves, and streams of air are then used to force open the shells and release the nibs.

TREASURES

Frances Boswell made her name as a food stylist and food editor for Martha Stewart's *Living* where she earned a reputation for making realistic recipes look inspirational on the page. Boswell went on to be food director of *Real Simple* for several years. She is currently on a break from the magazines – but continues to dabble with her favorite foods and people. Boswell co-authored a children's food book with her mother-in-law, Elisabeth Luard perfectly titled *Food Adventures* (Kyle Books). Try these amazing Chocolate Caramel Puddings to sample the "happy" tastes of chocolate and caramel. Cook the puddings until they are just set; they will continue to set on cooling, but will remain super creamy in texture. So good!

CHOCOLATE

CARAMEL PUDDINGS

Preparation time: 20 minutes
Cooking time: 15-20 minutes
Use: eight $^1/_2$ cup ramekins or small heatproof glasses
Makes: 8

$^3/_4$ cup sugar

1 cup whole milk

$1^1/_2$ cups heavy cream

1 vanilla bean, split open and seeds removed

8 ounces dark chocolate, minimum 70% cocoa solids, finely chopped

pinch of salt

5 large egg yolks

Preheat oven to 325°F.

Heat ½ cup sugar in a heavy bottomed saucepan over a medium heat – let stand, without stirring, until sugar melts to form a dark amber color, about 5 to 6 minutes. You may need to swirl the pan around a bit, but do not stir with a spoon or spatula.

When sugar turns to amber caramel, gradually add the milk and 1 cup of the heavy cream – reduce heat and let simmer until all the caramel has dissolved. Add the vanilla seeds, chocolate and salt. Stir until chocolate melts. Remove from the heat and set aside.

Meanwhile, whisk together remaining sugar and egg yolks in a separate bowl. Whisk for about 3 to 5 minutes until the mixture is very thick and creamy. You should be able to leave a trail on the surface when the whisk is lifted from the mixture.

Add caramel to egg yolk mixture, working slowly to temper. Whisk together to combine. Ladle about ½ cup of batter into 8 small glasses or ramekins. Transfer to a deep roasting pan and fill with hot water coming about half way up the sides of the glasses. Carefully transfer the tin to the oven and bake for 15 to 20 minutes. The puddings will still be slightly wobbly, but they will set once cooled. Lift out of the water bath, and set aside to cool.

Either chill for 1 hour before serving or store in a very cool place until needed. Whip the remaining cream, and spoon on top of each pudding just before serving.

HINT: There are two ways of making caramel. This is the trickier method but is the fastest (the second method is on page 58). Make it easier by adding ¼ cup water to the sugar.

Strictly, these aren't really tuiles as the original golden "tuiles" are named after the tiles that dominate the rooftops of Provence, and, although these Chocolate Tuiles still bear the curved shape, their color has changed. They are the perfect accompaniment to ice cream or a chocolate mousse.

CHOCOLATE

TUILES

Preparation time: 10 minutes
Chilling time: 1 hour
Cooking time: 15 minutes
Use: three non-stick cookie sheets,
Makes: 12

1 large egg

1 large egg white

¹/₂ cup confectioners' sugar

3 tablespoons all-purpose flour

2 tablespoons organic unsweetened cocoa powder

1 teaspoon heavy cream

2 tablespoons unsalted butter, melted and cooled

1 cup pine nuts and slivered hazelnuts

If cookie sheets are not non-stick, line with silicon mats.

Whisk together the egg and the egg white in a bowl. Sift in the confectioners' sugar, flour, and cocoa. Stir to mix well. Add the cream, and melted butter and mix until smooth. Stir in the pine nuts and slivered hazelnuts.

Place heaped tablespoons of the mixture onto the non-stick trays, leaving plenty of room in between, and refrigerate for 1 hour.

Preheat the oven to 350°F.

Dip a fork in warm water and, shaking off any excess water, flatten the mixture into discs using the back of the fork.

Bake for 10 minutes or until the "tuiles" are firm and have an even color. Remove from the oven and immediately place them over a rolling pin to give them a curved shape. Let cool and store in an airtight container.

HINT: The "tuiles" look wonderful served upside down, overlapping one another in rows in the same way as they would be laid on a roof in the south of France.

If you need to make this recipe for more than six people, double the quantities but use two separate pans – it begins to look like a great beast if you make one enormous one! This healthier version of a meringue roulade which uses yogurt instead of cream is delicious with almost any fruit but looks especially effective if you use green and red grapes or any berries.

MERINGUE ROULADE
WITH CHOCOLATE

Preparation time: 30 minutes
Cooking time: 45 minutes
Use: 15 x 11-inch baking pan
Serves: 6–8

ROULADE

4 large egg whites

1 cup superfine sugar

2–3 tablespoons confectioners' sugar for dusting

2 tablespoons organic unsweetened cocoa powder

2$^1/_4$ cups whole milk yogurt

one 3.5-ounce bar dark chocolate, minimum 60% cocoa content, chopped into small chunks

11 ounces raspberries (about 2 cups)

RASPBERRY COULIS

8 ounces raspberries (about 1$^1/_2$ cups)

$^1/_3$ cup confectioners' sugar

Cut out two sheets of parchment paper so that the sides rise about 2 inches from the bottom of the baking sheet. Butter the baking pan, and then line it with one piece of the parchment paper. Reserve the other piece.

Preheat the oven to 200°F.

Whisk the egg whites until soft peaks form. Continue to whisk, gradually adding half the sugar. Continue to whisk until the mixture is stiff but not dry. Fold in the remaining sugar.

Spoon the meringue into the prepared pan, spreading it evenly into the corners. Bake for 40 to 45 minutes, until it is tinged with color and firm yet spongy when pressed. Let cool for about 1 hour.

To make the coulis, purée the raspberries in a blender and then strain into a bowl. Stir in the confectioners' sugar to taste.

Place the large sheet of parchment paper on a clean surface and sift over the confectioners' sugar and cocoa. Turn the baked meringue (still in its paper) upside down onto the dusted paper. Remove the baking pan. Carefully peel away the paper from the meringue.

Spread the yogurt over the meringue. Scatter the chocolate chunks evenly over the yogurt and then scatter the raspberries evenly on top. Very carefully roll up the roulade using the paper as a support. Save any leftover sugar and cocoa for sprinkling over the roulade before serving. Chill in the refrigerator until required. Do not freeze for more than 5 hours. Serve with the raspberry coulis.

HINT: Do not worry about the meringue cracking slightly as you roll it up – it will look beautiful once you have sprinkled the leftover confectioners' sugar and cocoa over it.

Jo Gilks gave up her lucrative job in the City of London for food. She has always loved to cook and has forged a very different, yet often equally stressful, career for herself as a chef. Her Chocolate Pecan Pie has become a Thanksgiving dinner favorite.

JO'S CHOCOLATE

PECAN PIE

Preparation time: 35 minutes plus 25 minutes chilling
Cooking time: 1 hour, 25 minutes
Use: 11-inch removable-bottomed fluted tart pan
Serves: 8–10

PASTRY DOUGH

2 cups all-purpose flour

²/₃ cup confectioners' sugar

²/₃ cup (1¹/₄ sticks) unsalted butter, chilled

2 large egg yolks

2–3 tablespoons cold water

FILLING

10 ounces dark chocolate,
minimum 60% cocoa content, broken into pieces

2 cups shelled pecans, chopped

3 large eggs, beaten

1 firmly packed cup light soft brown sugar

1 cup evaporated milk

1 teaspoon pure vanilla extract

¹/₄ cup (¹/₂ stick) unsalted butter, melted

Sift the flour and confectioners' sugar into a large bowl. Cut in the butter until the mixture forms large crumbs. Mix the egg yolks and water and mix into the flour mixture to form a dough. Form the dough into a disc and cover with plastic wrap. Refrigerate for up to 1 hour.

On a floured surface, roll the dough into a 13-inch circle. Transfer to the tart pan and trim the edges. Pierce the base all over with a fork. Chill for 30 minutes. Preheat the oven to 375°F.

Line the pie shell with parchment paper or foil, fill with dried beans, and bake for about 20 minutes.

Remove the beans and paper and return the pie crust to the oven for another 5 minutes or until it is lightly colored. Transfer crust to a wire rack to cool slightly. Set aside while preparing the filling.

Reduce the oven temperature to 325°F.

Melt the chocolate in a heatproof bowl set over a saucepan of simmering water. Mix together all the remaining ingredients for the filling, then stir in the melted chocolate. Spoon into the pie shell and return it to the oven for 1 hour until the filling is set and the top looks crusty. Cool for at least 2 to 3 hours.

HINT: Any dried beans or legumes can be used for blind baking – red, kidney, or black beans, corn or rice – all they are doing is putting weight on the pie crust so that it doesn't rise during baking. Once cooled, they can be used again and again.

MYSTICAL

Hurricane Iris hit Belize on October 21st 2001. It destroyed many homes and crops and caused havoc for the cacao that survived, but more cacao trees have since been replanted by the growers. This cacao pod has been bored into by a woodpecker.

The drama of a soufflé straight from the oven will always stir a table of dinner party guests. Remember the success of a soufflé is in the rising, so take note of the hints at the bottom of the page. This is another of our trusted tester, Jo Gilks's, foolproof recipes.

CHOCOLATE SOUFFLÉ
WITH TOFFEE SAUCE

Preparation time: 20 minutes
Cooking time: 10–15 minutes
Use: six 2¹/₂-inch ramekins or custard cups
Serves: 6

1 teaspoon unsalted butter

1 tablespoon sugar

1 tablespoon organic, unsweetened cocoa powder

SOUFFLE

4 ounces dark chocolate,
minimum 60% cocoa **content**, broken into pieces

³/₄ cup organic unsweetened cocoa powder

8 large egg whites

¹/₄ cup superfine sugar

TOFFEE SAUCE

one 3.5-ounce bar toffee chocolate,
broken into pieces

4 tablespoons milk

Preheat the oven to 375°F.

To prepare the ramekins, melt the butter and brush the insides of the ramekins. Mix the sugar with the cocoa and sprinkle into each ramekin until coated, shaking out any excess. Chill until required.

Melt the chocolate in a heatproof bowl set over a saucepan of simmering water. Remove bowl from pan.

Mix the cocoa with ²/₃ cup of cold water in a saucepan, then bring to a boil whisking continuously. Boil for 10 seconds. Mix the cocoa mixture into the melted chocolate.

Prepare the Toffee Sauce so that it will be ready when you serve the soufflé. Melt the chocolate with milk in a small saucepan over a very low heat until the chocolate and toffee pieces are melted and combined with the milk. Remove from heat.

Continue with the soufflés by whisking the egg whites in a large bowl until soft peaks form. Add the sugar and continue whisking until stiff peaks form. Add one-quarter of the beaten whites to the cocoa mixture and whisk until thoroughly blended. Gently fold in the remaining egg whites using a metal spoon to cut through the whites as you fold so that you do not knock the air out of it.

Fill each prepared ramekin to the rim with the soufflé mixture and, using a butter knife, level off the surface. Run your thumb around the rim of each ramekin, pushing away the soufflé mixture, so that it does not stick to the edge and will rise evenly.

Bake the soufflés for about 10 to 15 minutes. Remove from the oven and pour a little Toffee Sauce over each soufflé and serve immediately.

HINT: When brushing the ramekins with the melted butter, brush from the bottom of the ramekin up towards the rim – this seems to help the soufflé to rise evenly. Remember not to open the oven door while the soufflé is cooking or the rush of cold air may prevent it from rising as high as you would wish.

Chocolate pudding is loved by all. Call it a mousse, syllabub or custard - it's all a type of pudding. Here are just a few more to add to your repertoire.

HILARY METH'S
EGGLESS MOUSSE

Chilling time: minimum 2 hours.
Serves: 4–6

two 3.5-ounce bars dark chocolate, minimum 60% cocoa content, broken into pieces

1³/₄ cups canned coconut milk

2 gelatin leaves or ¹/₂-package granulated gelatin

2 tablespoons confectioners' sugar

2 teaspoons pure vanilla extract

Melt the chocolate in a heatproof bowl set over a saucepan of simmering water. In another pan, gently heat the coconut milk, add the gelatin, and stir until dissolved. Sift the confectioners' sugar and add to the coconut milk, stirring to dissolve. Finally, stir in the vanilla and chocolate. Transfer to a large serving bowl and chill for at least 2 hours until set. Dust with cocoa, and decorate with toasted coconut flakes to serve.

LIGHT AND DARK
MOUSSE

Chilling time: minimum 1 hour.
Serves: 6

two 3.5-ounce bars dark chocolate, minimum 60% cocoa content, finely chopped

¹/₄ cup whole milk

2 large egg yolks

¹/₂ teaspoon vanilla extract

4 large egg whites

3 tablespoons superfine sugar

Melt the chocolate and milk in a heatproof bowl set over a saucepan of simmering water. Stir together until smooth. Remove bowl from pan. Stir the egg yolks into the chocolate until well blended, then stir in the vanilla. In a large bowl, whisk the egg whites until soft peaks form. Add the sugar gradually and continue to beat until stiff and glossy. Stir a ladleful of egg whites into the chocolate mixture to lighten it, then gently fold in the rest of the egg whites. Transfer the pudding into a serving bowl. Chill for at least 3 hours until just set. Decorate with grated chocolate to serve.

HINT: Always use eggs at room temperature. Do not overbeat egg whites and remember to use a clean bowl. Use the melted chocolate while it is still warm to the touch. Do not let the melted chocolate and egg yolk mixture cool down too much, otherwise it will be difficult to mix in the egg whites.

WHITE CHOCOLATE, CARDAMOM MOUSSE

NIGEL SLATER'S

Chilling time: 4 hours.
Serves: 6–8

8 plump green cardamom pods

¹/₂ cup milk

3 bay leaves

9 ounces good-quality white chocolate, broken into pieces (about 1¹/₂ cups)

1¹/₄ cups whipping cream

3 large egg whites

cocoa powder for dusting

Crack open the cardamom pods and extract the seeds. Crush seeds with a pestle and mortar. Put the milk, crushed cardamom seeds and bay leaves in a small saucepan; bring to just below boiling point. Remove from the heat, cover and set aside for 10 minutes. Strain. Melt the chocolate in a heatproof bowl set over a saucepan of simmering water. Remove bowl from pan. Whip the cream to form soft peaks. In another bowl, whisk the egg whites until stiff peaks form. Mix the chocolate and milk together until velvety. Stir a spoonful of the egg whites into the chocolate mixture, then gently fold in the remaining egg whites using a large metal spoon. Gently fold in the softly whipped cream. Spoon into individual glasses and refrigerate for 4 hours. Dust with cocoa just before serving.

DARK CHOCOLATE MOUSSE

WITH COFFEE

Chilling time: at least 6 hours.
Serves: 6

5 ounces dark chocolate,
minimum 60% cocoa content, broken into pieces

2 tablespoons fresh brewed coffee

1/4 cup (1/2 stick) plus 1 tablespoon unsalted butter

3 large eggs, separated

3 tablespoons sugar

cocoa powder

Melt the chocolate with the coffee and butter in a heatproof bowl set over a saucepan of simmering water. Stir until smooth. Remove bowl from pan. Stir in the egg yolks until the mixture is very smooth. In a bowl, whisk the egg whites until soft peaks form, add the sugar, and beat until the mixture is stiff and glossy. Fold a ladleful into the chocolate then fold in remaining egg whites delicately, ensuring no white spots from the meringue remain. Spoon into a serving bowl or 6 individual serving cups and chill for at least 6 hours. Dust with cocoa powder to serve.

A French family gave Angela Dempsey this recipe in the Seventies. She has since added the black currants and honey which has confirmed its position as her family's favorite pudding.

BITTER CHOCOLATE MOUSSE
WITH BLACK CURRANTS

Chilling time: minimum 1 hour.
Serves: 4–6

1/4 cup of black currants topped and tailed or canned black currants, strained

2 teaspoons honey

5 ounces Hazelnut and Currant Dark Chocolate or other good-quality fruit and nut chocolate, broken into pieces (about 1 cup)

5 large egg whites

2 tablespoons superfine sugar

2 large egg yolks

Over a gentle heat, soften the black currants with the honey for 3 minutes. Remove from the heat and let cool. Melt the chocolate in a heatproof bowl set over a saucepan of simmering water. Remove bowl from pan. In a large bowl, whisk the egg whites until soft peaks form, then add the sugar. Continue to whisk until stiff and glossy. Stir the egg yolks into the melted chocolate then mix in one-third of the egg whites. Gently fold in the remaining egg whites. Spoon the black currants into the base of 6 serving cups or glasses, then pour in the chocolate mousse. Chill for at least 2 hours before serving.

SIMPLE WHITE MOUSSE

Chilling time: minimum 4 hours.
Serves: 4–6

four 3.5-ounce bars good-quality white chocolate, broken into pieces (about 2–2 1/2 cups)

3 gelatin leaves

3 cups whipping cream

5 large egg yolks

1 cup confectioners' sugar

3–4 tablespoons Grand Marnier

Melt the chocolate in a heatproof bowl set over a saucepan of simmering water. Dissolve the gelatin in two tablespoons of warmed cream. Beat the egg yolks and sugar until doubled in volume and thickened, add the Grand Marnier, gelatin cream, and melted chocolate, and stir together well. Whip the remaining cream until thick and then fold into the chocolate mixture. Pour into a mold or individual ramekins and chill for 4 hours. This mousse is delicious served with a raspberry coulis or with a crust of melted dark chocolate, poured on top and left to harden.

HINT: Remember to use a metal spoon when folding in the egg whites and to cut through the mixture as you fold. This way you do not knock the air out of the beaten whites and the mousse remains light and fluffy.

Rachel Green runs her own business cooking for four to four hundred people. She has cooked many times for the Royal Family. A farmer's daughter from Lincolnshire, Rachel is dedicated to supporting and promoting regional producers.

CHOCOLATE AND LEMONGRASS

MOUSSE

Chilling time: 2 hours
Serves: 6

3 sticks of lemongrass

1 cup whole milk

10 ounces milk chocolate,
preferably 34% cocoa content, broken into pieces

1¹/₂ gelatin leaves or ¹/₂-package granulated gelatin

¹/₄ cup granulated sugar

1¹/₄ cups heavy cream

Finely chop the lower 3 inches of each stalk of lemongrass or grind in a food processor. Pour the milk into a saucepan, add the lemongrass, and bring to a boil. Remove from the heat, cover, and let infuse for 1 hour. Melt the chocolate in a heatproof bowl set over a saucepan of simmering water. Strain the milk discarding the lemongrass pulp. Return to a clean pan. Whisk the sugar and gelatin into the milk and return to a low heat, stirring continuously until the gelatin has melted and sugar dissolved. Remove from the heat and stir in the melted chocolate. Allow to cool down completely. Whip the cream in a bowl until it begins to thicken, but it should not be too stiff. Gently fold into the chocolate mixture. Spoon the mousse into a large serving bowl or 6 individual glasses. Chill for 2 hours to set. Serve.

HINT: Look for plump lemongrass stalks. If they look dry, discard. The flavor is in the bulb part of the stalk. Use only the 3 inches at the base. Lemongrass freezes well. Wrap in plastic wrap then a resealable bag to freeze. Use straight from the freezer.

This is one of those recipes that people either love or hate. It is irresistible if you are addicted to Toblerone or like a sweet mousse, and is the ultimate test of whether you have a sweet tooth.

CHOCOLATE NOUGAT
MOUSSE

Chilling time: 6 hours
Serves: 6

10$\frac{1}{2}$ ounces Toblerone, broken into pieces, reserving one piece for decoration

6 tablespoons hot water

1$\frac{1}{4}$ cups crème fraîche or sour cream

2 egg whites

Melt the chocolate and water in a heatproof bowl set over a saucepan of simmering water. Stir until smooth. Remove bowl from the pan. Leave to cool then fold in crème fraîche. In a bowl, whisk the egg whites until stiff peaks form; fold into the chocolate. Chill for at least 6 hours. Transfer to a serving bowl.

Once removed from the bean, the nibs are then roasted at over 100°C (212°F) to develop the rich flavor and characteristic color of cocoa.

The roasted nibs are then ground to produce cocoa liquor (or cocoa mass) which is made up of cocoa particles suspended in 50 to 55 percent cocoa butter.

The cocoa liquor is then transformed into chocolate by further processing and the addition of other ingredients. It can also be separated into cocoa powder and liquid cocoa butter.

"Cocoa content" is the term used to describe the total amount of cocoa-derived material in a finished chocolate. The percentage of cocoa content declared on chocolate packaging can refer to a combination of cocoa liquor and extra cocoa butter, as in most chocolate bars, cocoa butter in white chocolate, or just cocoa liquor, but this is rarely used on its own.

Cocoa Butter

Cocoa Liquor

Cocoa Powder

Rick Bayless is one of America's foremost practitioners of Mexican cooking. Bayless and his wife, Deann Groen Bayless, own and operate the highly acclaimed Chicago restaurants Frontera Grill and Topolobampo. There are many variations of flan, the classic being the dark caramel surface set on a milky-vanilla baked custard. This version is adapted from Bayless's book, *Mexican Kitchen* (Scribner), replacing the Mexican cinnamon chocolate with a dark chocolate with a high cocoa content, and infusing the milk with cinnamon – to put back that customary cinnamon-chocolate combo.

MEXICAN

CHOCOLATE FLAN

Preparation time: 20 minutes plus 30 minutes infusing
Cooking time: 25 minutes
Use: six 5-6 ounce custard cups
Makes: 6

1/2 cup plus 1/3 cup granulated sugar

1 cup half-and-half

1 cup whole milk

4 1/2 ounces dark chocolate,
minimum 70% cocoa content, finely chopped

two 2 inch cinnamon sticks, preferably Mexican

4 large eggs

1 tablespoon Kahlúa or other coffee liqueur

1/2 teaspoon pure vanilla extract

1/4 teaspoon pure almond extract

Set six 5 to 6 ounce custard cups into a baking pan deep enough to hold about 2 inches of water.

Put 1/2 cup of the sugar into a small heavy saucepan, add 1/4 cup water and set over a low heat. Stir until the sugar dissolves. Without stirring, bring to the boil and continue to boil for 5–8 minutes until a deep amber caramel is formed. Working quickly and carefully, divide the caramel between the cups, swirling to evenly spread the caramel on the bottom and a little up the sides of the cups. Set aside.

For the custard, pour the half-and-half and milk into a saucepan and set over a low heat. Add the chocolate,

cinnamon sticks and remaining sugar to the milk, and continue to heat, stirring until the sugar dissolves and the chocolate melts. Remove from the heat, cover and leave to infuse for 30 minutes.

Position the oven rack to the center of the oven. Preheat the oven to 325°F.

Whisk the eggs, Kahlúa, vanilla and almond extracts in a bowl. Gradually whisk in the warm milk mixture. Strain through a fine-mesh sieve into a large measuring jug or pitcher, discarding the cinnamon. Divide the mixture between the custard cups.

Pour about 2 inches of hot water into the pan, surrounding the custard cups. Lay a sheet of foil over the top of the pan, but do not seal. Transfer to the oven and bake for 25 minutes, the custard will have barely set. Remove from the oven, but let the custards cool in the water bath, where they will continue to set. Once cold, refrigerate the custards for 1–2 hours until thoroughly chilled. They can be chilled overnight.

To unmold, run a thin-bladed knife or small metal spatula around the edge of the mold, ensure the knife has gone all the way to the bottom of the cup. Twist the mold back and forth to make sure that the custard moves freely. Invert a serving plate over each mold, then reverse the two and listen for the flan to drop.

HINT: The flans can be made up to 3 days in advance and kept refrigerated.
Unmold as required. In fact, the longer the flans are chilled, the easier they are to remove from the cups.

Inspired by the popularity of tarts, Isobel Wakemen transformed her reliable Chocolate and Seville Orange Mousse into this Moorish Tart. Seville oranges are in season around February, recognised by their thicker skins and bitter flavor.

MOORISH
TART

Preparation time: 30 minutes
Cooking time: 40 minutes
Chilling time: 3 hours
Use: 8-inch fluted tart pan

PASTRY DOUGH

1¹/₃ cups all-purpose flour

¹/₃ cup confectioners' sugar

¹/₂ cup (1 stick) plus 1 tablespoon unsalted butter

grated zest of 1 Seville orange
(reserve the orange for the filling)

1 large egg, beaten

FILLING

5 ounces dark chocolate,
minimum 60% cocoa content, broken into pieces

1 cup heavy cream

4 large egg yolks

¹/₄ cup firmly packed light brown sugar

juice of 1 Seville orange

Preheat the oven to 375°F.

To make the dough, blend the flour, confectioners' sugar, butter, and orange zest in a food processor to the breadcrumb stage, or rub the ingredients together between your fingers. Add the beaten egg and mix until a dough forms. Cover with plastic wrap and chill for 30 minutes.

Roll out the dough on a lightly floured board and line the tart pan. Trim excess pastry and prick the bottom with a fork. Chill for 30 minutes. Line the crust with foil and fill with baking beans, bake for 20 minutes, then remove the beans and the foil and continue to bake for another 10 minutes. Remove from the oven and let cool.

Melt the chocolate with the cream in a bowl set over a saucepan of simmering water. Remove bowl from pan.

To make the filling, beat the egg yolks and sugar until light and fluffy. Give the melted chocolate and cream a stir, then add the egg mixture to the chocolate. Return bowl to the pan of simmering water and stir until the mixture thickens. Add the orange juice and stir for 2 to 3 minutes or until the mixture thickens again. Do not let the mixture boil. Pour into the cooled pie shell and chill until set, about 3 hours.

HINT: Seville oranges freeze well, so if using right from the freezer, grate the zest before thawing.

KUKUH

OR XOCOLATL

Theobroma, the genus that all cacao trees belong to, literally means "food of the gods" from the Greek *theos* for "god" and *broma*, meaning "food or drink." The Swedish naturalist Carolus Linnaeus named the tree in the eighteenth century in tribute to the Maya and Aztec drink.

In Mexico, cocoa beans served as currency and the "food of the gods" was also at the heart of many rituals and ceremonies. This heady, aromatic, cocoa beverage, *xocolatl* or *kukuh*, was favored by Montezuma, the sixteenth-century king of the Aztecs, who drank it as a potent aphrodisiac. A simple infusion, it is spiced with chile and thickened with ground corn.

On a recent trip to Belize, Cluny Brown, our marketing manager, was given a bowl of *kukuh* and was told how to make this refreshing, slightly watery drink. Cocoa beans are roasted on a *comal*, a smooth griddle, until their skins fall away, then they are ground together with a little corn and ground black pepper or dried, toasted chile pepper. A little sugar is usually added, although in ancient times the Maya used forest honey. The drink can be served hot, tepid, or cold, and given the extreme heat and humidity in Belize, it is delicious chilled and very different from the Western version we enjoy on cold winter days.

Auzibio Sho, who works at the Toledo Cocoa Growers Association in southern Belize, claims that not only is it good for general well-being, it is also great for inducing labor as well. *Kukuh* is also consumed for health and energy and is given to sick people and those who need to work hard.

To make this revitalizing drink yourself, take a handful of cocoa beans and toast them on a griddle. Crack open the shells and remove the cocoa nibs. Grind the nibs in a mortar and pestle to a smooth paste and then stir in some freshly ground black pepper and ground corn. Take about a teaspoon of the paste and add enough water to make a large glass. Sweeten with sugar to taste. The Maya vary this drink by adding spices such as cinnamon, allspice, and nutmeg.

HINT: Be warned. *Kukuh* is a very different drink to our traditional
sweet and creamy hot chocolate drink.

This cake is light and moist, and the flavor of the chocolate and the almonds together with the texture and taste of the figs combine to make it truly unforgettable. Rachael Vingoe sent us this recipe, inspired by a cake that she bakes each Christmas.

CHOCOLATE, FIG, AND ALMOND
CAKE

Preparation time: 20 minutes
Baking time: 50 minutes
Use: 9-inch springform cake pan

5 ounces dried ready-to-eat figs (about 1 cup)

3 tablespoons Amaretto

3 ounces ground almonds (about $^1/_3$ cup)

$^3/_4$ cup all-purpose flour

1 cup plus 2 tablespoons ($2^1/_4$ sticks) unsalted butter, softened

$1^1/_4$ cups granulated sugar

4 large eggs, beaten

two 3.5-ounce bars dark chocolate, minimum 60% cocoa content, chopped

3 heaped tablespoons organic unsweetened cocoa powder

4 ounces blanched almonds (about $^3/_4$ cup)

Preheat the oven to 350°F. Butter and line the cake pan with parchment paper. Alternatively, butter the pan and dust with ground almonds to coat, shaking out any excess.

Discard the hard stalks from the figs and chop in a food processor into very small pieces. Place in a small bowl and stir in the Amaretto. Set aside.

Mix the ground almonds with the flour in a separate bowl. Beat the butter and sugar until light and fluffy. Gradually add the eggs, beating well between each addition. Then add the almonds and flour, a third at a time, continuing to beat gently.

Carefully fold in the chopped chocolate, the figs, and Amaretto to the batter.

Spoon the batter into the cake pan and smooth the surface with a small metal spatula. Sieve the top evenly with 2 heaped tablespoons of cocoa. Arrange the almonds on top and then bake the cake for 40 to 50 minutes or until it is firm to the touch and a skewer inserted in the center comes out clean. Cool on a wire rack. Dust surface with remaining cocoa to serve.

HINT: Serve with freshly chopped coconut stirred into whipped cream.

If you are ever in Paris, treat yourself to tea in the beautiful dining rooms at Ladurée on the Champs Élysées. Don't be put off by the lines of people waiting and don't leave without an exquisitely wrapped box of the most famous macaroons in Paris.

CHOCOLATE
MACAROONS

Preparation time: 20 minutes
Cooking time: 10–12 minutes
Use: 2 large cookie sheets, large pastry bag with $^3/_4$-inch nozzle

$4^1/_2$ ounces ground almonds (about $1^1/_3$ cups)

$^1/_4$ cup organic unsweetened cocoa powder

$2^1/_4$ cups confectioners' sugar

3 large egg whites, at room temperature

$^1/_4$ teaspoon pure vanilla extract

2 tablespoons cocoa powder for dusting

FILLING

use any of the truffle mixtures on pages 145 or 147

Preheat the oven to 475°F.

Line the cookie sheets with parchment paper with an overlap of about an inch at either end. Prepare your pastry bag and nozzle.

Put the ground almonds in a bowl. Sift in cocoa, and 2 cups of confectioners' sugar.

Measure out exactly a scant half-cup of the egg whites, setting aside any excess whites for another use.

In a large bowl, whisk the egg whites until they are light and fluffy, sift in the reserved confectioners'

sugar and continue to whisk until they are stiff and shiny but not dry. Gently fold the dry ingredients into the egg whites. Let rest for 10 minutes.

Stir the vanilla extract into the mixture, allowing it to deflate a little. This will help to stop the macaroons from cracking on top. Pour the mixture into the pastry bag. Pipe the mixture onto the cookie sheets in balls each about the size of walnuts. Tap the bottoms of the cookie sheets on a flat surface to remove some more of the air from the macaroons. Sift some cocoa on top of each one.

Put the first cookie sheet on the top shelf of the oven and bake for 1 minute, and then reduce the temperature to 350°F. Cook the macaroons for another 10 to 12 minutes or until they are set, smooth and shiny; they should be soft to the touch.

About 1 minute after you have removed the cookie sheet from the oven, gently lift one end of the paper and immediately pour a splash of hot water under the paper. The hot baking sheet causes the water to form steam and makes it easy to remove the macaroons. Carefully peel the macaroons from the paper and place on a wire rack to cool. Repeat the process with the second batch.

Once the macaroons have cooled, sandwich two together with the truffle filling.

HINT: The secret is to use "old" egg whites that have been kept uncovered in a refrigerator for at least a week.

Dodi Miller is passionate about chiles and is the driving force behind the company that has made the greatest variety and best-quality chiles available in the UK. She is also passionate about her Mole Poblano recipe and explains that it is a dish that can take a couple of days to prepare and that it is made for people you love, usually for festive occasions. There are many moles: green, red, yellow, and black, but Poblano, the one with chocolate, is the most famous. The chocolate is used as a spice; it rounds off the edges of the chiles and gives the sauce a deep richness.

COOL CHILE Co.

MOLE POBLANO DE GUAJOLOTE

(dark chile, nut, and chocolate mole with turkey)

Preparation time: 2 hours
Cooking time: 1$\frac{1}{2}$ hours. Best left for a day before eating
Use: stockpot, large ovenproof pan
Serves: 8–10. For 12–16 use a 9–11 pound turkey and double the quantities for the mole

5–6$\frac{1}{2}$ pound turkey (or a large chicken; the long slow cooking suits robust free-range birds)

STOCK INGREDIENTS

1 onion

1 carrot

1 stalk celery

1 bay leaf

dried thyme

salt

pepper

MOLE

1 large beef tomato, skinned, blackened on a grill pan, core removed

2 tablespoons sesame seeds, dry toasted

2 tablespoons coriander seeds, dry toasted

1$\frac{1}{2}$ ounces dark chocolate, minimum 60% cocoa content, grated (about $\frac{1}{2}$ cup)

4$\frac{1}{2}$ ounces dried mulato chiles

1$\frac{1}{2}$ ounces dried ancho chiles

1$\frac{1}{4}$ ounces dried pasilla chiles

$\frac{1}{3}$ cup duck/goose fat or lard, melted, or vegetable oil

$\frac{1}{3}$ cup whole almonds, skin on

3 tablespoons raisins

1 small onion, peeled and chopped

2 garlic cloves, peeled and chopped

2 whole cloves (or pinch of ground clove)

5 peppercorns (or $\frac{1}{4}$ teaspoon ground black pepper)

$\frac{1}{2}$ teaspoon ground cinnamon

2 stale corn tortillas or 2 stale pieces bread (or use 2 tablespoons masa harina)

1 teaspoon salt

2 tablespoons sugar

$\frac{1}{4}$ teaspoon ground anise (or 1 star anise)

sesame seeds, for garnishing

Ask your butcher to cut up the turkey, saving the carcass, trimmings, and giblets to make the stock. You can also do this yourself: remove the wings, legs, thighs, and breasts with the bones in, wrap, and keep in the refrigerator. Put the carcass, wing tips, and giblets into a stockpot, cover with water, add the stock ingredients, simmer for 2 hours, partially covered, then skim and strain to produce a rich, tasty stock.

To make the mole, chop the roasted tomato and put it into a bowl, along with the toasted sesame and coriander seeds and the grated chocolate.

To prepare the dried chiles, wipe off any dirt with a barely damp cloth. Pull out the stem and run your finger down the side to open the chile out flat, shake out all the seeds, and remove the membranes attaching them. Make a pile of the flat chile pieces. Heat 2 tablespoons of the melted fat or oil in a skillet over medium-high heat. Fry the chile pieces one at a time for just a few seconds on either side; the color will become tan. Do not overdo this, as the chiles will become very bitter. Drain as much of the fat back into the pan as you lift out the chiles and put them into a separate bowl. When you have finished frying all the chiles cover them with just boiled water using a weighted bowl to keep them submerged. Put to one side and soak for 1 hour, then drain.

Add a little more fat in the skillet, if necessary, and toast the almonds until golden, drain and add to the bowl containing the chopped tomato. Sauté the raisins until they puff, drain them and add to the bowl. Add the onions and garlic to the skillet and sauté until brown, drain and add to the bowl. Add the cloves, black pepper, and cinnamon to the pan, fry for one minute and then add them to the bowl as well. Finally tear the stale corn tortillas into pieces, fry, drain, and add them to the bowl. Or if using masa harina, scoop out a little of the tomato mixture and mix the masa harina into it and then stir it back into the bowl.

Put a quarter of the tomato mixture and about $\frac{1}{3}$-cup of stock into a blender and blend until smooth. Strain into a clean bowl and continue blending the tomato mixture and stock, adding only enough stock to produce a thick paste, until the tomato mixture is used up.

Drain the chiles. Purée chiles in 4 batches, adding $\frac{1}{3}$-cup stock to each batch so they blend easily. Strain into a separate bowl.

Pat the turkey pieces dry using paper towel. Heat two tablespoons of the melted fat or oil in a Dutch oven and brown the turkey on all sides, working in batches if necessary. Drain on paper towels.

When complete, drain away most of the fat, leaving a little, and reheat. Add the chile purée, stirring all the time, letting it bubble, darken and thicken. This takes about 5 minutes. Then add the tomato-based purée and simmer for about 2 minutes. Add 3 cups of the stock, reduce the heat and simmer the sauce for 45 minutes. Then add a teaspoon salt and 2 tablespoons sugar, or to taste. The sauce should coat the back of a spoon – add a little more stock if it is too thick.

Preheat the oven to 350°F. Return the turkey to the pot, coat with the sauce, add the anise or star anise, cover and transfer to the oven for 1 hour and 30 minutes until the turkey is tender.

Serve sprinkled with toasted sesame seeds. Be generous with the sauce over the turkey.

HINT: Serve with rice, corn tortillas and a fresh watercress salad.

WICKED

The rain forest is the perfect environment for the cacao tree, which likes rich soil, humidity, and shade.It is rare to fi
Theobroma cacao growing outside a band 20 degrees north and 20 degrees south of the Equator.

David Lebovitz received much of his training at Alice Waters' world-famous restaurant Chez Panisse in Berkeley, California. He spent over 12 years in the pastry department helping to create desserts to complement seasonal menus. David now lives in Paris leading chocolate tours throughout Europe in between writing several dessert books such as *The Great Book of Chocolate* and his latest, *The Perfect Scoop*.

CHOCOLATE

RUM AND RAISIN SOUFFLÉ CAKE

Preparation time: 30 minutes plus soaking for 1 hour
Cooking time: 1 hour
Use: 9-inch spring form pan
Serves: 12-16

$^2/_3$ cup raisins, chopped, or dried currants

$^1/_2$ cup dark rum

butter for greasing

12 ounces dark chocolate, minimum 70% cocoa content, chopped

$^3/_4$ cup heavy cream

5 large eggs, at room temperature

pinch of salt

$^1/_2$ cup superfine sugar

In a small saucepan, heat the raisins or currants with the rum until it begins to boil. Simmer for 1 minute. Remove from heat, cover, and let stand for at least one hour.

Preheat the oven to 325°F. Lightly butter a 9-inch spring form pan and wrap the outside of the pan with aluminum foil, to make it watertight. Set the cake pan in a large roasting pan.

Put the chopped chocolate with $^1/_2$ cup cream in a large heatproof bowl. Strain the rum from the raisins into the chocolate, pressing to extract as much rum as possible. Set the raisins aside. Put the chocolate over a saucepan of simmering water, stirring gently until melted, about 5 to 8 minutes. Note, mixture will not be super smooth, do not worry. Remove the bowl from pan.

In a separate bowl whip the remaining cream until it forms peaks when you lift the whisk. Fold the whipped cream into the melted chocolate.

In a clean bowl, add the egg whites, salt, and sugar and whip on high speed until they hold their shape, about 5 minutes. Using a rubber spatula, fold half of the eggs whites into the chocolate, then the raisins or dried currants, then the remaining eggs.

Scrape the batter into the prepared cake pan. Add warm water to the roasting pan so that it reaches half-way up the sides of the spring form pan.

Bake for 1 hour, until the cake is slightly firm, but will still feel soft in the center. Do not be tempted to over bake, as the cake will become firmer on cooling. Remove the cake pan from the water bath and set on a cooling rack until it becomes room temperature. Slice to serve.

HINT: Run a knife along the inside of the cake pan to release the cake from the pan. Lift off the outside ring of the spring form cake pan. Because the cake is delicate, it's best sliced with a thin, sharp knife dipped in very hot water and wiped clean before making each slice.

WICKED

White Chocolate

When we make our Dark Chocolate with 70% cocoa content, we begin by mixing together cocoa liquor, raw cane sugar, and Bourbon vanilla to our own special recipe.

This mixture is then refined through a series of rollers that grind the particles of cocoa, sugar, and vanilla so finely that they cannot be felt on the tongue. This process also continues to develop the flavor of the chocolate.

The next stage is the conching, which cannot be hurried and is a vital stage in the production of quality chocolate. A conching vessel, named after the conch shell-shape of the first prototype, controls the temperature and stirs the chocolate to create a smooth, velvety texture. The volatile acids are driven off and the flavor of the chocolate matures.

The ultimate indulgence after a cold walk, this recipe can be made simpler by omitting the cinnamon or the cream but the drink will be less rich.

LUXURY

COCOA

Preparation time: 15 minutes
Makes: 1 standard mug

1 cup whole milk

2 tablespoons heavy cream

2 sticks cinnamon, about 2 inches long

1 tablespoon organic unsweetened cocoa powder

about 2 teaspoons unrefined cane sugar
(or sugar of your choice)

Put the milk, cream, and cinnamon sticks in a pan and slowly bring to a boil. Remove from heat, cover and let infuse for 10 minutes.

When you are ready to serve the cocoa, remove cinnamon sticks. Reheat the milk, spoon the cocoa powder into a large mug, add enough of the milk mixture to form a paste, and stir.

When the milk mixture has just reached scalding point, pour into a mug, stirring to blend the cocoa paste with the milk. Add sugar to taste, and stir well.

Serve with cinnamon sticks.

HINT: If you like cardamom, try substituting the cinnamon with the black seeds
from inside one or two green cardamom pods, slightly crushed with the back of a spoon.
Let the seeds infuse for 10 minutes before reheating, then strain the mixture into the mug.

Seek out good-quality white chocolate made with real vanilla and cocoa butter. Children love this sweet recipe from Jenny Phillips. This recipe can be baked in a 2-pound loaf pan. Bake for 50 minutes. Simply drizzle with the white chocolate and omit the filling.

BANANA
AND WHITE CHOCOLATE CAKE

Preparation time: 20 minutes
Cooking time: 35 minutes
Use: two 7-inch cake pans

CAKE

³/₄ cup (1¹/₂ sticks) unsalted butter

³/₄ cup granulated sugar

3 large eggs, beaten

2 ripe bananas, mashed

2 cups self-rising flour
(if you do not have self-rising flour, then use all-purpose flour, increase the baking powder to 3¹/₂ teaspoons, and add 1 teaspoon salt.)

¹/₂ teaspoon baking powder

FILLING

2 ripe bananas

juice of 1 lemon

1 tablespoon rosewater

²/₃ cup crème fraîche or sour cream

ICING

two 3.5-ounce bars good-quality white chocolate, broken into pieces

3 tablespoons unsalted butter

Preheat the oven to 350°F. Brush the cake pans with melted butter and dust with flour.

Beat together the butter and sugar until light and fluffy. Gradually beat in the eggs and mashed banana. Sift the flour and baking powder, in 2 batches, into the mixture and fold in well.

Divide the batter between the 2 pans and bake for about 40 minutes until well risen. Leave the cakes in the pans for 10 minutes, then turn out onto a wire rack to cool.

To make the filling, thinly slice the bananas and toss in the lemon juice. Mix the rosewater into the crème fraîche and spread this onto one of the cooled cake layers, top with the sliced bananas, and sandwich with the remaining cake.

Melt the white chocolate and the butter in a heatproof bowl set over a saucepan of simmering water. Stir until smooth.

Spread the melted chocolate mixture evenly over the top and sides of the cake, starting by pouring it into the center of the top of the cake and spreading it with a metal spatula until it begins to dribble down the sides of the cake.

Hint: If liked, decorate the cake with edible flowers. Violets and pansies are the easiest to find.

What would we do without those little books crammed with recipes from enthusiastic cooks compiled to raise money for schools and charities? This recipe, from the Bergvliet Road Nursery School in Cape Town, South Africa, has that Sixties ring to it – it is sweet and very rich and, along with a cup of tea, is guaranteed to hit the spot.

COFFEE, CHOCOLATE
AND WALNUT CAKE

Preparation time: 25 minutes
Cooking time: 25 minutes
Use: two 7-inch round cake pans
Serves: 10

2 cups (4 sticks) unsalted butter

1 cup firmly packed light brown sugar

4 large eggs

1 cup minus 2 tablespoons strong fresh brewed coffee, cooled

4 teaspoons organic, unsweetened cocoa powder

1²/₃ cups self-rising flour

1¹/₂ cups walnuts, chopped

walnuts for decorating

FROSTING
Nigella's Blond Icing (see page 181)

Preheat the oven to 375°F. Butter and flour the two pans.

Beat the butter and sugar until light and fluffy, add the eggs, one at a time, beating well between each addition. Mix in the coffee. Sift the cocoa and self-rising flour together and add to the mixture, beating well. Don't worry if the mixture has curdled slightly as it will come together once baked. Fold in the chopped walnuts and divide the mixture between the two pans, level the surface.

Bake in the oven for 25 minutes. Let cool in the pans for a few minutes before turning out on to a wire rack to cool completely.

When the cakes have cooled, place one cake on a serving plate and frost the top and sides. Place the other cake on top and frost its top and sides. Decorate with walnut pieces.

Hint: If liked, turn walnuts into a crunch praline and sprinkle over the cake. Put ½ cup granulated sugar in a heavy based pan, heat over medium heat until sugar dissolves and turns a deep amber caramel. Stir in ¼ cup chopped walnuts. Pour onto greased cookie sheet. Leave to cool. Remove from cookie sheet and chop.

WICKED

After working as a cook and professional caterer, Melissa Clark earned an MFA in writing from Columbia University and has written 18 cookbooks. Her latest: *The Skinny: How to fit into your little black dress forever* (Meredith). Imagine everybody's pleasant surprise when they cut into their traditional Thanksgiving pie to find melted chocolate. What a good idea!

BLACK BOTTOM

PUMPKIN PIE

Preparation time: 30 minutes + chilling of pastry
Cooking time: 1 hour 10 minutes
Use: One 9-inch pie plate
Serves: 8 to 10

FOR THE CRUST

1 cup all-purpose flour

$^1/_2$ teaspoon salt

6 tablespoons ($^3/_4$ stick) cold unsalted butter, or shortening, or a combination, cut into cubes

2 to 3 tablespoons cold water, as needed

FOR THE FILLING

One 15-ounce can pumpkin purée

1 cup heavy cream

3 large eggs, beaten

$^3/_4$ cup firmly packed light brown sugar

2 tablespoons dark rum or brandy

$1^1/_2$ teaspoons ground cinnamon

$1^1/_2$ teaspoons ground ginger

$^1/_4$ teaspoon ground allspice

$^1/_4$ teaspoon salt

$2^1/_2$ ounces dark chocolate, minimum 70% cocoa content, coarsely chopped

Whisk together the flour and salt in a large bowl. Cut in the butter and/or shortening until the mixture forms large crumbs. Sprinkle the water, 1 tablespoon at a time, over the mixture and toss gently with a fork until the dough just comes together without crumbling apart. Form the dough into a disc, cover with plastic wrap, and refrigerate for at least 1 hour and up to 2 days.

Preheat the oven to 375°F.

On a floured surface, roll the dough into an 11-inch circle. Transfer it to a 9-inch pie plate and crimp the edges. Line the crust with parchment paper and fill with pie weights or dried beans. Bake for 20 minutes, then remove the paper and weights from the crust. Continue baking a further 5 minutes more. Transfer crust to a rack to cool slightly.

Reduce oven temperature to 325°F.

In a large bowl, whisk together the pumpkin purée with the cream and eggs until smooth. Whisk in the brown sugar, rum, spices and salt, taking care that the mixture is smooth and there are no lumps of brown sugar.

Scatter the chocolate over the bottom of the crust. Pour over the pumpkin mixture. Bake until the filling is just set, about 45 minutes. It will seem wobbly in the center, but it is perfect. Cool for 2 hours before serving.

HINT: Do not be tempted to bake the pie filling until it looks completely set; otherwise on cooling the custard will contract and cause a great big crack in the center of the pie.

"You may lose the thread of your thoughts when you savor one of these sun-filled Mediterranean dates," writes Marialuisa Rea Faggionato from Padua in Italy. She stuffs the dates with an orange- and lemon-flavored marzipan, coats them in dark chocolate, and serves them chilled for dessert. Marialuisa was a runner-up in one of our recipe competitions.

MEDITERRANEAN

THOUGHT-STEALING DATES

Preparation time: 30 minutes
Cooling time: 30 minutes
Use: wire rack
Makes: 30

30 Medjool dates

$^1/_2$ cup blanched whole almonds

$^1/_4$ cup superfine sugar

finely grated zest of 1 orange,
plus a little of the juice

4 teaspoons Limoncello
(Italian liqueur flavored with lemon zest)

5 ounces dark chocolate,
minimum 60% cocoa content, broken into pieces

Remove the pits from the dates. Put the almonds in a food processor and chop finely. Add the sugar and orange zest, and Limoncello. Process until a dough forms, adding a little orange juice if needed. Shape the marzipan and use to stuff the dates.

Melt the chocolate in a heatproof bowl set over a saucepan of simmering water. Remove the bowl from the pan. Dip the ends of the dates into the chocolate, leaving the center bare, or dunk them to coat completely. Dip them twice if you like. Leave them in a cool place to set. Serve.

HINT: Try to use fresh dates for this recipe, but if you can't find them, choose dates that have been coated in as little syrup as possible.

Hazel Neil likes to adapt recipes depending upon seasonal availability and the contents of her pantry. Next time she will try plums.

CHOCOLATE, PEAR, AND GINGER

TART

Preparation time: 40 minutes
Chilling time: 30 minutes
Cooking time: 1 hour
Use: 11-inch removable-bottomed fluted tart pan
Serves: 8

PIE DOUGH

2 cups all-purpose flour

$^1/_2$ teaspoon salt

$^1/_2$ cup (1 stick) unsalted butter, diced

2 large egg yolks

4–5 tablespoons cold water

FILLING

$^1/_2$ cup (1 stick) unsalted butter

$^1/_2$ cup sugar

2 large eggs

one 3.5-ounce bar dark chocolate, minimum 60% cocoa content, broken into pieces

1 tablespoon finely chopped preserved ginger in syrup

3 tablespoons all-purpose flour

$1^1/_3$ cups ground almonds

4 pears, just ripe, peeled

apricot jam for glaze

Preheat the oven to 375°F.

To make the pie dough, sift the flour and salt into a large bowl. Rub the butter into the flour using your fingers until it resembles bread crumbs. In a small bowl, whisk together the egg yolks and the cold water then add to the mixture. Mix together to form a dough. Cover the dough in plastic wrap and chill for about 30 minutes, roll out. Use dough to line your tart pan, trim excess pastry. Prick base with a fork. Line crust with parchment paper and fill with dried beans. Bake for 20 minutes. Remove paper and return crust to oven for a further 5 minutes.

Reduce oven temperature to 325°F.

To make the filling, beat the butter and sugar until light and fluffy. Gradually beat in the eggs. Melt chocolate in a heatproof bowl set over a saucepan of simmering water. Stir until smooth. Remove bowl from pan. Mix in the chocolate and ginger. Fold in the flour and the almonds. Spoon into pie crust.

Cut the pears in half, remove the cores, and slice into wedges. Arrange in a fan shape on top of the chocolate mixture and press in slightly. Bake for 30 to 40 minutes. Test that the filling is cooked by inserting a skewer into the center which should come out clean.

Brush with apricot jam while still warm and serve warm or cold, with chocolate sauce (see page 60) or cream.

Andrea Longman invented these crumbly and buttery slices for a vegan friend as a thank-you present. They are now a regular feature of her Christmas cookie cooking bonanza and are her friend's favorite Christmas present. If you make these for children, use milk chocolate instead.

SCRUMMY
CHOCOLATE SWIRL SHORTBREAD

Preparation time: 20 minutes
Cooking time: 25 minutes
Use: 2 cookie sheets
Makes: 14

SHORTBREAD 1

1 cup all-purpose flour

$1/2$ teaspoon salt

$1/4$ cup granulated sugar

$1/2$ cup (1 stick) unsalted butter or vegan margarine

SHORTBREAD 2

1 cup all-purpose flour

$1/4$ cup organic unsweetened cocoa powder

$1/2$ teaspoon salt

$1/4$ cup sugar

$1/2$ cup (1 stick) unsalted butter or vegan margarine

one 3.5-ounce bar dark chocolate,
minimum 60% cocoa content, or milk chocolate,
preferably 34% cocoa content, finely chopped

Preheat the oven to 300°F. Line 2 cookie sheets with parchment paper.

To make the first shortbread, sift the flour, salt, and sugar into a bowl. Rub in the butter until the mixture combines. Knead lightly, then place the dough in the refrigerator for 30 minutes before rolling out.

Follow the same step for the second shortbread, but include the cocoa with the flour.

Roll out each dough on a lightly floured surface into equal-sized rectangles about $1/2$-inch thick. Place the plain shortbread on a sheet of waxed paper, place the chocolate shortbread on top of the plain one and then scatter the chocolate all over.

Carefully roll the shortbread, as tightly as possible, using the waxed paper to support it. (Don't worry if it breaks or the chocolate pokes through.) Once rolled, pinch both ends together to prevent the chocolate falling out, then using both hands, squeeze until it is about 8 inches long.

Using a very sharp knife, slice the roll into $1/2$-inch slices. Lay the cookies on the cookie sheet, 2 inches apart. Bake for 25 minutes, until the plain shortbread is a light golden color. Cool on a wire rack.

HINT: The cookies are delicious eaten slightly warm with the chocolate still half melted. If liked, chill prepared cook log for up to 3 hours or overnight. Slice and bake as required.

Julie Hasson, through her experience as a commercial baker and caterer, has developed a distinctive style that can best be described as minimum fuss with maximum results. Her belief is that cooking should be enjoyable, exciting, and offer a reprieve from everyday stress and pressure. Hasson has three books on chocolate published and one on cupcakes. The recipe below is adapted from her book *300 Best Chocolate Recipes*. These delectable cookies are absolutely sublime with the addition of a dark chocolate and high in cocoa content. "I crave these cookies as much as I crave my morning coffee", she confesses.

CHOCOLATE CHUNK
ESPRESSO COOKIES

Preparation time: 20 minutes
Cooking time: 15–20 minutes
Use: 2 cookie sheets
Makes: 18

3 cups all-purpose flour

1 tablespoon ground cinnamon

$^{1}/_{2}$ teaspoon baking soda

$^{1}/_{4}$ teaspoon salt

1 cup (2 sticks) unsalted butter, room temperature

1$^{1}/_{2}$ cups firmly packed light brown sugar

2 teaspoons pure vanilla extract

1 teaspoon grated orange zest

1 large egg

4 teaspoons instant espresso or coffee crystals

10 ounces dark chocolate, minimum 70% cocoa content, chopped into chunks

Preheat the oven to 350°F. Line cookie sheets with parchment paper.

In a large bowl, mix together the flour, cinnamon, baking soda and salt. Set aside.

In a large bowl or bowl of an electric stand mixer, beat together the butter and brown sugar until light and fluffy. Beat in vanilla and grated orange peel. Add the egg and instant espresso, beating until smooth. Add the flour mixture, mixing just until blended. Stir in chocolate chunks.

Scoop dough into $^{1}/_{4}$-cup size balls and place on prepared cookie sheets, 2 inches apart. Slightly flatten tops and bake for 15 to 20 minutes, or until puffed but still slightly soft to the touch. Cool cookies on cookie sheets before transferring to a rack to cool.

HINT: Add $^{3}/_{4}$ cup toasted walnut or pecan pieces along with the chocolate chunks.

Lee Napoli has been dubbed Boston's most well-known and beloved pastry queen. Napoli practices her craft as the Pastry Chef at South End Buttery, Boston, MA.

These truffles have quite an exceptional smooth texture (the extra cocoa butter). Coat the final truffles with tempered chocolate and then a dusting of cocoa again. Try serving the truffles with Warres LBV Port 1995 or 2005 Boekenhoutskloof Chocolate Block.

CHOCOLATE
ESPRESSO TRUFFLES

Preparation time: 1 hour
Chilling time: 2 hours and 45 minutes
Makes: 34

1 pound baking chocolate, chopped into pieces

2 tablespoons cocoa butter

2 cups heavy cream

$^1/_4$ cup sugar

coffee liqueur

cocoa powder and confectioners' sugar, for dusting

Put the chocolate into a heatproof bowl with the cocoa butter. Set aside.

Combine the heavy cream and sugar in a small saucepan and heat until scalded. Do not boil.

Pour scalded cream and sugar over chocolate and cocoa butter in bowl. Let sit for 3 to 5 minutes. Whisk smooth, mixture should be shiny. Gradually add the coffee liqueur, whisking after each addition.

Transfer truffle mixture to a shallow pan, cover and refrigerate till firm enough to scoop, about 2 hours.

Once the truffle mixture is firm enough to scoop, shape the mixture into 34 small balls, using either a small melon-baller, teaspoon measurer or small sorbet scoop. Place the balls on a cookie sheet and return to the refrigerator for another 30 minutes.

To coat the truffles with tempered chocolate, work quickly. With a deep soup spoon in one hand, scoop up some tempered chocolate, add the truffle, and move around with a fork in your other hand. Once coated, lift the truffle with the fork, drain, allowing the drips of excess chocolate to fall back in the bowl. Return to the cookie sheet. Chill once more for 15 minutes. Coat lightly with sifted cocoa powder to finish. Serve.

HINT: It is important to sift cocoa powder to remove any lumps that happen naturally in its container.

Dina Cheney is the author of *Tasting Club* (DK Publishing). She is a freelance writer and tasting host. These truffles are so simple to make – just infuse cream with lavender and fennel, combine with chocolate and a bit of butter (for an extra smooth, velvety texture), chill, form into balls, and roll in cocoa powder. For variations, feel free to substitute other flavoring ingredients for the lavender and fennel. For instance, try fresh mint leaves, earl grey tea leaves, or even curry powder.

FRESH CHOCOLATE TRUFFLES
WITH LAVENDER AND FENNEL

Preparation time: 25 minutes
Chilling time: 2 hours and 30 minutes
Makes: about 28 small truffles

$^1/_2$ teaspoon whole fennel seeds

6 ounces Green & Black's Organic Dark Chocolate with 70% Cocoa Solids

$^2/_3$ cup heavy cream

2 tablespoons unsalted butter, diced

1 teaspoon pesticide-free dried lavender

2 tablespoons granulated sugar

$^1/_4$ cup organic unsweetened cocoa powder

Place the fennel seeds in a small, heavy skillet over medium-high heat. Toast the seeds until fragrant, about 3 minutes (watch carefully, so they don't burn). Using a spice grinder or mini-food processor, grind to a fine powder, about 30 seconds. Set aside.

In a food processor, grind the chocolate to a fine powder, about 10 seconds. Pour ground chocolate into a medium-sized, heatproof bowl, and set aside.

Place the cream and butter in a small, heavy saucepan and bring to a boil over high heat, about 1–2 minutes. Once boiling, remove from heat and stir in the lavender and fennel seeds. Cover and steep for 10 minutes.

Strain the infused cream into the bowl with the ground chocolate, pressing on the solids in the strainer with the back of a spoon. Discard solids remaining in the strainer. Add the granulated sugar to the chocolate-cream (ganache) mixture. Whisk the chocolate, cream, and sugar together until smooth. If not completely smooth, place the bowl over a pan of simmering water to help melt the chocolate a little more. Cover the bowl with plastic wrap and refrigerate for about 2 hours until the mixture is thick enough to scoop.

When ready to form truffles, sieve the cocoa powder into a small- to medium-sized bowl to break up any clumps. Set the large platter that you'll be using for storing the truffles next to it. Remove the ganache from the fridge.

Using a teaspoon melon baller or teaspoon measurer and your hands, form balls out of the ganache. Dredge the balls in the cocoa, shake off any excess, and place the finished truffles on the platter. Continue making truffles until all of the ganache has been used up.

Chill truffles for 30 minutes or more, and serve.

HINT: The required amount of sugar can vary depending on the brand and cocoa precentage of the chocolate used. If you substitute Green & Black's chocolate with an equivalent brand that contains more sugar, it is likely you will not need to add the additional 2 tablespoons of sugar.

The complex flavor of chocolate is created by 550 flavor compounds found in cocoa after fermentation, drying, roasting, and conching – far more than in most foods. A carrot has 96 flavor compounds.

TEMPERING

To mold chocolate or cover a cake in a hard chocolate shell that will set with a glossy shine, you have to temper the chocolate first, in exactly the same way we mold our chocolate bars.

Tempering involves melting, cooling, and then reheating the chocolate, ensuring that all the tiny fat crystals in the chocolate are stable. If the fat crystals are not stable, the chocolate will set with white streaks or bloom. It will also be dull and won't have a good snap – the sound that good chocolate makes when you break it.

HOW TO TEMPER CHOCOLATE

To temper chocolate you need to use a minimum of $10\frac{1}{2}$ ounces of dark, milk, or white chocolate (three 3.5-ounce bars). Any excess can always be stored and re-used another time.

Grate about $\frac{1}{2}$-cup of chocolate and set it aside. Break the remainder of the chocolate into pieces and melt in the top of a double boiler over gently simmering water; if using the alternative method described on page 9, do not let the bottom of the bowl come into direct contact with the water. Once the chocolate is completely melted, check the temperature using a digital thermometer. It should be between 131 and 136°F for dark chocolate, and between 113 and 122°F for milk and white chocolate.

Remove the chocolate from the heat and place over a bowl of cold water at about 70°F. Let cool, while occasionally stirring, until the temperature of the chocolate drops to 93°F.

Gently stir in the reserved grated chocolate and continue stirring until all the chocolate has melted and the temperature has cooled to 89 to 91°F.

The final temperature for dark chocolate should be about 86 to 90°F, between 82 to 86°F for milk, and 82 to 84°F for white chocolate.

To test whether you have tempered your chocolate correctly, dip the tip of a butter knife in the chocolate and then let it cool and set for about 5 minutes. Properly tempered chocolate will be smooth with an even color on the top, and if you peel the chocolate off the knife, the bottom will appear shiny. You can always start again using the same chocolate if you have failed to temper it properly.

Use the tempered chocolate immediately and quickly, leaving it over a pan of warm water while you work with it.

For a less technical method, see page 9.

ABRACADABRA

This impressive, rich, chocolate cake is incredibly easy to make and guaranteed to launch your guests into orbit. It can also be made by replacing some of the dark chocolate with Maya Gold Chocolate, to give the cake a hint of orange and spice. For an extra-special occasion, shake or brush edible gold dust (available from specialty cooking stores) over it.

DARK CHOCOLATE MOUSSE CAKE

WITH GOLD DUST

Preparation time: 10 minutes
Cooking time: 35–45 minutes
Use: 8- or 9-inch springform cake pan with removable base or a similar-sized removable-bottomed tart pan
Serves: 10

1 tablespoon ground almonds, plus extra for dusting the pan

three 3.5-ounce bars dark chocolate, minimum 60% cocoa content
or two 3.5-ounce bars dark chocolate and one 3.5-ounce bar Maya Gold Chocolate, or other good-quality dark, orange-flavored chocolate, broken into pieces

1¹/₂ cups granulated sugar

²/₃ cup (1¹/₄ sticks) unsalted butter

pinch of sea salt

5 large eggs

confectioners' sugar or gold dust

Preheat the oven to 350°F. Brush the pan with a little melted butter and dust with the ground almonds, shaking off any excess.

Melt the chocolate, sugar, butter, and salt in a heat-proof bowl set over a saucepan of simmering water. Stir until smooth. Remove bowl from pan.

Beat the eggs with 1 tablespoon ground almonds and fold into the chocolate mixture. The batter will thicken after a few minutes. Pour into the cake pan and bake for 35 to 40 minutes.

Remove the sides of the pan and leave the cake on the bottom part to cool, then dust using a small sieve with confectioners' sugar or brush with edible gold dust.

HINT: This cake will not rise much – it should be rich and light.
If chilled overnight it will be dense, fudgey, and wicked!

Micah Carr-Hill, our chocolate taster and product development chef, came back from one of his many forays in Italy with this dreamy idea. He visited the "Salone del Gusto," a food fair that takes place in Turin every other autumn, and spent one evening at a dinner that had a chocolate theme. Make sure your Gorgonzola dolce is perfectly ripe, not too runny and not too hard, and don't be afraid to pile on the chopped chocolate. The idea is that you taste the Gorgonzola first and then the chocolate begins to melt in your mouth and cuts through the richness, leaving you in a state of calm ecstasy.

GORGONZOLA DOLCE

WITH DARK CHOCOLATE

Preparation time: 5 minutes
Makes: 60 pieces

one 3.5-ounce bar dark chocolate, minimum 60% cocoa content

12 ounces Gorgonzola dolce

Chop the chocolate into medium-sized chunks, about the size of your thumbnail, using a serrated bread knife.

Cover the entire surface of the cheese with the chunks of chocolate, pressing it in gently.

Make sure that the cheese is densely covered, as you do need a high proportion of chocolate to cheese to get the full benefit of this recipe.

HINT: Try to avoid wrapping cheeses with plastic wrap. Ideally they should be covered with wax paper then foil. Store in an airtight container in the refrigerator. Bring the cheese back to room temperature before serving.

Lori Longbotham, the New York based desserts cookbook author and ex-gourmet food editor, knows her chocolate. This classic pound cake is adapted from her cookbook, *Lucious Chocolate Desserts* (Chronicle). The special element to this chocolate pound cake recipe is that it is made with real chocolate rather than cocoa powder. It can be cooked in a regular cake pan or bundt pan. Serve with a chocolate sauce or ice cream.

CHOCOLATE

POUND CAKE

Preparation time: 35 minutes
Cooking time: 1 hour and 15 minutes
Use: 7-inch bundt pan
Serves: 8 to 10

extra butter and flour for greasing
and flouring pan

1 cup flour

¹/₄ cup finely ground almonds

4 ounces dark chocolate, minimum 60% cocoa
content, chopped

5 tablespoons water

¹/₂ cup (1 stick) unsalted butter,
at room temperature

¹/₂ cup granulated sugar

2 large eggs, separated

1 large egg white

¹/₄ teaspoon salt

Position rack in the middle of the oven. Preheat oven to 325°F. Rub the inside of the bundt pan with butter. Swirl a few teaspoons of flour around to coat completely. Invert the pan and tap out the excess. Place in a roasting tin (do not add water yet).

Sift the flour into a large bowl and stir in the ground almonds. Set aside.

Put the chocolate and water in a heatproof bowl. Set the bowl over a saucepan of simmering water and stir until melted, about 5 to 8 minutes. Remove the bowl from the pan; set aside.

Put the butter and sugar in a large bowl and beat with an electric mixer for about 5 minutes, until light and fluffy. Gradually add the egg yolks, beating well between each addition. Add the chocolate and beat well. Fold in the flour mixture in 2 batches, scraping down the sides of the bowl with a rubber spatula to make sure all the ingredients are incorporated.

In a clean bowl, whisk egg whites and salt with clean beaters until stiff peaks form. Fold a quarter of the egg whites into the chocolate mixture to loosen a little. Then fold in the remaining egg whites. Transfer the cake batter to the prepared pan and level the surface.

Fill the pan with enough hot water to come halfway up the sides of the cake pan. Bake 1 hour 15 minutes, or until a cake tester comes out clean. Remove the pan from the water and let it cook on a wire rack for 10 minutes. Turn onto the wire rack and let cool. Serve cut into wedges with caramel chocolate sauce (see page 58) or with fresh whipped cream.

HINT: This is a good basic recipe to have. Bake the cake in a 9-inch square cake tin for 45 minutes. Cut into squares and decorate each individually for a party or cake stand sale.

A great classic, this recipe was picked up in the Eighties in Paris and originated in the famous Taillevent restaurant. It is delicious served with Mint Crème Anglaise (see page 60) and Chocolate Tuiles (see page 106).

TAILLEVENT

TERRINE

Preparation time: 20 minutes
Freezing time: overnight
Use: 1-pound loaf pan

8 ounces dark chocolate,
minimum 60% cocoa content, broken into pieces

1 cup confectioners' sugar

³/₄ cup (1¹/₂ sticks) softened unsalted butter

5 large eggs, separated

1 cup organic unsweetened cocoa powder, sieved

salt

³/₄ cup whipping cream

Melt the chocolate in a heatproof bowl set over a saucepan of simmering water. Stir until smooth. Remove bowl from pan.

Stir the confectioners' sugar into the chocolate. Add in the softened butter, follwed by the egg yolks, cocoa, and a pinch of salt; beat until mixed.

In a separate bowl, whisk the egg whites until soft peaks form. In another bowl, whip the cream until thick. Fold the egg whites and the whipped cream into the chocolate batter, alternating in 2 batches each.

Sprinkle water inside the loaf pan, line with plastic wrap, pour the mixture into the pan, and freeze overnight. Remove from the freezer for about 15 minutes before required. Lift out of the loaf tin, and slice into ¹/₂-inch thick slices. Serve with Mint Crème Anglaise and Chocolate Tuiles.

HINT: This terrine can be kept in the freezer for up to a week.

ABRACADABRA

Whole Earth Foods was started by Craig Sams, one of the pioneers of the organic movement, who was extolling the beliefs of macrobiotics and organic farming over thirty-five years ago, when the majority of us had not even begun to think about the effects of conventional farming methods on the environment and our health. Cocoa Crunch, a naughty yet healthy breakfast cereal adored by adults and children alike, is one of the many delicious organic foods produced by Whole Earth.

COCOA
CRUNCH

Preparation time: 10 minutes
Cooking time: 35–40 minutes
Use: large roasting pan or baking pan
Makes: 1lb, 2oz

1^1/$_4$ cups granulated sugar

^{1}/$_2$ cup water

^{1}/$_4$ cup vegetable oil

3 ounces milk chocolate, preferably 34% cocoa content, chopped

2 teaspoons honey

3 heaped cups old-fashioned oats

4^1/$_2$ cups Rice Krispies (or puffed rice cereal)

^{1}/$_2$ cup dried shredded coconut

^{1}/$_3$ cup organic unsweetened cocoa powder

Preheat the oven to 350°F.

Line a large roasting or baking pan with parchment paper.

Dissolve the sugar in the water over low heat to make a syrup without caramelizing it. This takes about 5 minutes. Let the syrup cool until warm and then add the vegetable oil and chocolate, and stir to melt in the syrup. Add the honey to the syrup and mix well.

In a large bowl, mix together the oats, Rice Krispies, coconut, and cocoa. Add the syrup mixture to the dry ingredients and mix thoroughly. Spread the mixture onto the prepared baking pan to a thickness of about ^{1}/$_2$-inch.

Bake for about 35 to 40 minutes, and, using a fork, turn the Cocoa Crunch regularly. Be careful not to crush it into fine crumbs though; it should remain as chunks, like a granola.

It is better to undercook the Cocoa Crunch as it will burn easily, especially around the sides of the baking pan, so do watch it.

HINT: Dip the spoon you are going to use to measure the honey into a cup of hot water and wipe dry, to prevent the honey from sticking to the spoon.

This crumbly cookie from Brittany is a traditional plain butter cookie. Ensure to choose a well-flavored butter as this is the main flavor for the cookie. Look out for organic varieties or even the French butters with salt flakes.

BRETON
BUTTER COOKIES

Preparation time: 10 minutes
Chilling time: 15 minutes
Cooking time: 15–20 minutes
Use: 2¹/₂-inch fluted cookie cutter, 2 cookie sheets
Makes: 50

2³/₄ cups all-purpose flour

large pinch of salt

²/₃ cup granulated sugar

³/₄ cup plus 2 tablespoons (1³/₄ sticks) unsalted butter, chilled and diced

1 large egg, lightly beaten

¹/₂ teaspoon pure vanilla extract

two 3.5-ounce bars milk chocolate or 2 ounces each of milk, dark, Maya Gold (or good-quality, dark, orange-flavored chocolate), and white chocolate, broken into pieces for dipping

Preheat the oven to 325°F. Line 2 cookie sheets with parchment paper.

Sift together the flour and the salt. Add the sugar and butter and blend in a food processor or else rub between your fingertips until the mixture resembles bread crumbs. Add the egg and the vanilla and blend again or mix together with your hands, until the mixture comes together as a firm dough. Wrap in plastic wrap and chill for at least 15 minutes.

Roll out on a lightly floured board to a thickness of about ¹/₈-inch. Cut out the cookies using the fluted cutter.

Place on the cookie sheet and bake for 15 to 20 minutes or until light golden. Cool on a wire rack.

Once the cookies have cooled, melt the chocolate in a heatproof bowl set over a saucepan of simmering water. If using one flavor of chocolate only, select a bowl that you can fit your hand into so you can dip the cookies into it. If you are using a variety of flavors of chocolate, once you've melted each one, pour the individual chocolates onto separate small plates and dip the surface of each cookie in the chocolate before returning them to the wire rack to set.

The cookies can simply have one surface dipped in the chocolate or you could decorate further by drizzling with contrasting colored or flavored chocolate.

HINT: The most effective way of melting chocolate is to microwave it very slowly on medium in short bursts. To melt ¹/₃ cup chocolate pieces, microwave for 30 seconds, then continue in 10-second bursts, stirring in between each one.

Jo Gilks finds there are times when she can't wait to tuck into a meaty stew with someone, as so many of her friends seem to have become vegans or vegetarians or developed food allergies. This cake is part of the repertoire that enables her to feed them. Made with polenta, which is cornmeal rather than a flour, it satisfies all those people whose wheat-free diets prevent them from eating many of the chocolate recipes she would usually make.

POLENTA CHOCOLATE
CAKE

Preparation time: 25 minutes
Cooking time: 40 minutes
Use: 10-inch springform, deep-sided cake pan
Serves: 10

8 ounces dark chocolate,
minimum 60% cocoa content, broken into pieces

$1/2$ cup (1 stick) unsalted butter

5 large eggs, separated

$2/3$ cup granulated sugar

1 cup fine polenta (cornmeal)

$1/4$ cup dark rum

confectioners' sugar for dusting

Preheat the oven to 350°F. Butter the cake pan and flour it well to prevent sticking.

Melt the chocolate and the butter in a heatproof bowl set over a saucepan of simmering water. Stir until smooth. Remove bowl from pan. Beat the egg yolks with half of the sugar until the mixture is thick and creamy. Fold into the chocolate mixture.

In another bowl, whisk the egg whites with the remaining sugar until stiff peaks form. Stir the polenta and rum into the chocolate mixture then fold in the beaten whites.

Spoon the batter into the prepared cake pan and bake for about 40 minutes until it just shrinks from the sides. Remove from the oven and let cake cool in the pan (it will sink as it cools). Dust with confectioners' sugar before serving.

HINT: For a crisp crust, add all the sugar to the egg yolks
and whisk the egg whites without any sugar.

This tart, with its crumbly, buttery crust, is a cross between a cookie and a pastry and is very easy to make. It can be filled with almost anything, although we think our creamy chocolate spread is the perfect match for the pine nuts.

ITALIAN PINE NUT TART
WITH CHOCOLATE SPREAD

Preparation time: 35 minutes
Chilling time: 45 minutes
Cooking time: 30–35 minutes
Use: 9-inch removable bottomed fluted tart pan
Serves: 6–8

PASTRY DOUGH

2^1/$_4$ cups all-purpose flour

1 teaspoon baking powder

^{1}/$_3$ cup (^{3}/$_4$ stick) plus 1 tablespoon unsalted butter, cold, plus a little melted for greasing

^{2}/$_3$ cup granulated sugar

2 large eggs, beaten

about 2 tablespoons water

FILLING

11 ounces chocolate hazelnut spread (about 1^1/$_2$ cups)

TOPPING

1 large egg yolk

1 tablespoon milk

3 tablespoons pine nuts

1 tablespoon confectioners' sugar for dusting

Preheat the oven to 350°F. Lightly brush the inside of the tart pan with a little melted butter.

To make the dough, sift the flour and baking powder into a bowl and rub in the butter until the mixture resembles bread crumbs. Add the sugar and then mix in the eggs and some of the water. Mix together using your hands form a dough. Turn onto a lightly floured board and knead gently using the heel of your hand until the mixture is smooth and even. Cover with plastic wrap and chill for 45 minutes.

Roll out three-quarters of the dough on a lightly floured surface to an 11-inch circle. Use to line the tart pan and trim. Spoon the chocolate spread into the pie shell to cover it. Roll out the remaining dough and place it on top of the chocolate spread. Press the edges of the top and bottom crusts together to seal them.

To make the topping, beat together the egg yolk and milk, then brush it over the top crust. Sprinkle the pine nuts evenly on top of that and bake for 30 to 35 minutes until light brown. Dust with confectioners' sugar and let cool before serving.

HINT: Pine nuts burn very quickly so keep an eye on this tart during the later stages of baking. Cover with foil if browning too quickly.

ABRACADABRA

Elizabeth Karmel, the queen of the BBQ from North Carolina, really does know how to upgrade brownies. (Another of Karmel's recipes, Chocolate Kahlúa Walnut Pie, is on page 33.)

The sweet fruity flavor of the ancho chiles combined with the tart dried cherries works magically with the bittersweet chocolate. When you are making the brownies, remember that chiles vary in their heat quotient and you want to taste the chiles before grinding or chopping them. If they are really hot, reduce the quantity in the recipe. You want just a hint of heat – too much will kill the other flavors.

ANCHO CHILE
CHERRY BROWNIES

Preparation time: 30 minutes
Cook time: 40 minutes
Use: one 9-inch square brownie pan
Makes: 12 bars

8 ounces dark chocolate, minimum 72% cocoa content, roughly chopped

1/2 cup (1 stick) unsalted butter, plus more for greasing pan

2 large eggs

1 2/3 cups granulated sugar

2 teaspoons pure vanilla extract

1/2 teaspoon salt

1 cup all-purpose flour

3/4 cup dried cherries, chopped

2 small dried ancho chiles, roughly ground in a spice grinder or 1 1/2 teaspoons depending on the heat of the chiles

Preheat oven 350°F. Lightly grease the brownie pan and line the base with greased parchment paper.

Put 6 ounces of the chocolate in a heatproof bowl with the butter and place over a saucepan of simmering water. Melt until smooth, about 5 to 8 minutes, stirring occasionally.

In a large bowl, whisk the eggs, sugar, vanilla and salt until doubled in quantity and quite thick. You should be able to see a trail of mixture on the surface when the beaters are lifted out. Add the melted butter and chocolate. Gently fold in. Gradually add the flour, folding in well between each addition. Mix in cherries, the remaining chopped chocolate cherries and ground ancho chiles. Stir until batter is evenly mixed.

Pour the batter into the prepared brownie pan. Bake for 40 minutes or until the brownies are just pulling away at the sides. Allow the brownies to cool in the pan for several hours before cutting.

HINT: The center of the brownies should be moist but not runny – a little chocolate will cling to a cake tester when it is inserted in the middle. If you continue to bake, the brownies will be too dry.

This cake is incredibly quick and easy to make and the ground-up cinnamon stick topping reminds us of why we should always freshly grind our spices. Melody Talbot has lived in New York, London, Sydney, and Verbier and has always moved to her family's next destination with a batch of her favorite recipes. This coffee cake was scribbled on a scrap of paper at a gathering of mothers from her children's school in New York.

CHOCOLATE CHIP AND CINNAMON

COFFEE CAKE

Preparation time: 15 minutes
Cooking time: 50–60 minutes
Use: 9-inch springform cake pan
Serves: 8

TOPPING

2 cinnamon sticks or 1 teaspoon ground cinnamon

$^1/_3$ cup ($^3/_4$ stick) unsalted butter

$^1/_4$ cup granulated sugar

CAKE

$^1/_2$ cup (1 stick) unsalted butter, softened

1 cup granulated sugar

2 large eggs, beaten

$1^1/_4$ cups sour cream or whole milk yogurt

1 teaspoon pure vanilla extract

$3^1/_3$ cups self-rising flour
(or all-purpose flour with 4 teaspoons baking powder and 1 teaspoon salt added)

two 3.5-ounce bars dark chocolate,
minimum 60% cocoa content, chopped

Preheat the oven to 350°F. Butter and flour the cake pan.

To make the topping, grind the cinnamon sticks in a mortar and pestle or spice grinder. Melt the butter, add the sugar and the cinnamon, stirring well. Set aside.

To make the cake, beat the butter and sugar until light and creamy. Add the eggs, and continue to beat until smooth. Add the sour cream or yogurt, and the vanilla extract, and mix well. Sift in the flour and add the chocolate. Stir.

Pour the batter into the cake pan, then evenly spread the topping over the batter using the back of a spoon.

Bake for 50 to 60 minutes. Let cool in the pan before turning out.

HINT: Try to find cinnamon from Sri Lanka or the Seychelles. Avoid cassia, which is often passed off as cinnamon, but has a much cruder flavor and a tougher bark.

OLD TIMERS

The rain forest has existed for at least 40 million years and although it now covers just two percent of the earth's surface, 40 percent of all species of animals and plants live there. By 1990, half of the world's rain forests had been destroyed and they are still being felled at an alarming rate of about 54,800 square miles per year.

This wonderfully simple Kuglòf recipe was given to Csilla Fodor by her Hungarian grandmother, Eszter, who still lives in Oroshàza in south-eastern Hungary. Csilla has fond memories of spending summer holidays with her as a child when this cake, speckled with chocolate, was a great luxury after the bland food of her strict boarding school.

HUNGARIAN

KUGLÒF

Preparation time: 30 minutes
Cooking time: 55 minutes
Use: 8-inch kugelhof or bundt ring mold
Serves: 8

6 large eggs, separated

1³/₄ cups granulated sugar

³/₄ cup plus 2 tablespoons (1³/₄ sticks) unsalted butter, softened

3¹/₃ cups all-purpose flour

1 cup whole milk

1 teaspoon lemon juice

one 3.5-ounce bar dark chocolate, minimum 60% cocoa content, grated

confectioners' sugar for dusting

Preheat the oven to 275°F. Brush the inside of the ring mold thoroughly with melted butter. Dust with flour.

Beat together the egg yolks, sugar, and the butter. Sift the flour and add it to the batter, along with the milk and lemon juice, and mix well. In a large bowl, beat the egg whites until soft peaks form, then fold them gently into the batter. Divide the batter in half and add the grated chocolate to one of the halves.

Spoon the plain batter into the bottom of the ring mold, then top with the chocolate batter. Bake for about 55 minutes or until the kuglòf cracks slightly on the top.

Remove from the oven and let cool for about 10 minutes before turning out onto a wire rack. Once the kuglòf is completely cooled, dust with confectioners' sugar before serving.

HINT: To ensure the cake does not stick to the pan, place the ring mold in the freezer for 30 minutes before brushing it with butter and then dusting with flour.

Claire Fry is the graphic designer who has worked on both the Green & Black's and New Covent Garden Soup Company brands. She loves baking cakes and often makes elaborate themed ones for close friends. Her "Bandstand on Clapham Common" and "The Royal Albert Hall" were both wedding cakes for couples who enjoyed walking their dogs and singing in a choir. This recipe is the one she claims is infallible and lends itself to different shapes. It is delicious filled with apricot jam and covered with Toffee Bar or Chocolate Fudge Sauce.

DEVIL'S
FOOD CAKE

Preparation time: 15 minutes
Cooking time: 30–35 minutes
Use: two 8-inch round cake pans with deep sides
Makes: 10–12 large slices

$2^1/_2$ cups all-purpose flour

$^1/_2$ teaspoon baking powder

2 teaspoons baking soda

large pinch of salt

1 cup organic unsweetened cocoa powder

2 cups cold water

1 cup margarine or shortening

$2^1/_2$ cups granulated sugar

4 large eggs, beaten

7 ounces apricot jam (about $^3/_4$ cup)

Toffee Bar or Chocolate Fudge Sauce, see page 60

Preheat the oven to 350°F. Lightly grease the pans and line the bases with greased parchment paper.

Sift the flour with the baking powder, baking soda, and salt. Blend the cocoa with the water and set aside.

Beat the margarine or shortening until smooth. Add the sugar and beat until light and very soft. Gradually add the eggs beating well between each addition. Stir in the flour alternately with the blended cocoa water.

Divide the batter between the 2 pans and bake for 30 to 35 minutes or until a skewer inserted into the center comes out clean. Let cool for a few minutes in the pan, then turn out onto a wire rack to cool completely.

Sandwich the cakes with apricot jam or a filling of your choice. Pour Toffee Bar Sauce or Chocolate Fudge Sauce all over the top and well down the sides of the cake.

HINT: Don't be tempted to use butter when making this cake as it is definitely lighter and has a better texture made with margarine.

OLD TIMERS

Treat your friends to three different *pôts de crème*. They are exceedingly rich so why not serve them in egg cups, espresso cups or shot glasses on a dessert plate with a little coffee spoon and delicate Chocolate Tuiles (see page 106).

THREE PÔTS

DE CRÈME

Preparation time: 30 minutes
Chilling time: 2–3 hours
Use: egg cups or other small unusual containers – try liqueur glasses
Serves: 6

1³/₄ cups half and half

1 vanilla bean, split open with seeds scraped out

1 ounce dark chocolate,
minimum 60% cocoa content, broken into pieces

1 ounce Maya Gold Chocolate, or
other good-quality, dark, orange-flavored
chocolate, broken into pieces

2 ounces white chocolate, broken into pieces

6 large egg yolks

¹/₄ cup granulated sugar

¹/₂ teaspoon salt

Gently heat the half and half with the vanilla bean and seeds until bubbles begin to form at the edge, but make sure the cream does not boil. Remove from the heat, cover and set aside to infuse.

Melt the chocolates separately in heatproof bowls set over saucepans of simmering water. (Keep the saucepans of water as you will need them later on.) Remove the bowls from the heat and let the chocolates cool, then beat two of the egg yolks into each of the melted chocolates until the mixtures are smooth. Combine the sugar and salt, and stir one-third of the mixture into each chocolate mixture until completely dissolved.

Remove the vanilla bean from the cream and gently stir one-third of the cream into each chocolate mixture until well blended. Replace the bowls over the saucepans of simmering water.

Cook until each mixture coats the back of a spoon, stirring all the time.

Pour each chocolate mixture into your chosen containers and chill for about 2 to 3 hours or until the mixture has set.

HINT: Melt the chocolate before adding it to the cream. If you try to add chopped or grated chocolate to the hot mixture, it will seize and your pôts will be grainy.

Pastry chef Claudia Fleming learned her skills at Fauchon, in Paris. Fleming was then the pastry chef at prestigious Manhattan restaurants such as Montrachet, TriBeCa Grill, Luxe and Gremacy Tavern. Fleming and is known as the best pastry chef in New York. These brownie cookies are the perfect snack to have at hand.

CHOCOLATE
BROWNIE COOKIES

Preparation time: 30 minutes
Cooking time: in batches of 8 to 9 minutes (about 4 batches)
Use: 2 cookie sheets
Makes: 60 cookies

$^1/_4$ cup all-purpose flour

$^1/_4$ teaspoon baking powder

$^1/_8$ teaspoon salt

2 large eggs

$^3/_4$ cup granulated sugar

$^1/_2$ tablespoon brewed espresso

1 teaspoon pure vanilla extract

2 tablespoons unsalted butter

8 ounces dark chocolate, minimum 72% cocoa content, coarsely chopped

Preheat the oven to 375°F. Line 2 cookie sheets with parchment paper.

In a small bowl, sift together the flour, baking powder and salt. Set aside.

In the bowl of an electric mixer, whip the eggs to break them up. Add the sugar, espresso, and vanilla and beat on high speed for 15 minutes, until very thick.

While the eggs are whipping, place the butter in a heatproof bowl set over a saucepan of simmering water. Add 7 ounces of the chocolate to the bowl and heat until melted and smooth, about 5 to 8 minutes, stirring occasionally. Remove the bowl from the pan. Set aside.

Gently fold the chocolate mixture into the egg mixture until partially combined (there should still be some streaks). Add the flour mixture to the batter and carefully fold it in. Fold in the remaining chopped chocolate. If the batter is very runny, let it rest until it thickens slightly, about 5 minutes.

Drop the batter by heaping teaspoonfuls onto the prepared baking sheets and bake until puffed and cracked, 8 to 9 minutes. Cool on a wire rack before removing from the baking sheets.

HINT: If you do not have a standup mixer, put the egg mixture into a heatproof bowl and set over a saucepan of simmering water. Either use an electric hand whisk or a metal balloon whisk to whip the mixture until thick and trebled in volume.

This recipe will find a home for those sad, brown bananas that nobody wants to eat. An old favorite, it is the perfect coffee break treat and goes well with tea or coffee.

WHITE CHOCOLATE,
WALNUT, AND BANANA LOAF

Preparation time: 30 minutes
Baking time: 1–1¼ hours
Use: 2-pound loaf pan
Makes: 1 large loaf

½ cup (1 stick) unsalted butter, melted

1¼ cups all-purpose flour

2 teaspoons baking powder

½ teaspoon baking soda

½ teaspoon salt

⅔ cup granulated sugar

2 large eggs, beaten

4 small, very ripe bananas, mashed

one 3.5-ounce bar good-quality white chocolate, chopped into large chunks

½ cup walnuts, chopped

1 teaspoon pure vanilla extract

Preheat oven to 350°F. Brush the inside of the loaf pan with a little melted butter, then dust with flour.

Sift the flour, baking powder, baking soda, and salt in a bowl. In a separate bowl whisk the melted butter and sugar together. Beat in the eggs, one at a time, then beat in the mashed bananas. Add the white chocolate, walnuts, and vanilla. Add the dry ingredients to the banana batter in three stages, folding in after each addition.

Pour into the loaf pan and bake for 1 hour 15 minutes until loaf is well risen, golden and shrinks slightly from the side.

Loosen the sides of the loaf with a small metal spatula and leave it in the pan to cool.

HINT: Nigella's Blond Icing (see page 181) is delicious poured over this cake.

OLD TIMERS

You only have to spend a short time in the rain forest to understand why growing cacao organically makes sense. The cacao trees are planted under indigenous trees for shade, are sheltered from the wind and sun, and don't dry out when it gets too hot. Any insect pests that eat the crop are picked off by natural predators.

The forest floor is a carpet of leaf litter which fills the soil with the nutrients that help the plants to grow without any need of chemical fertilizers. This results in a bio-diverse environment where cacao trees thrive among forest flora and fauna.

Slashing and burning rain forest trees to intensify the cultivation of crops has destroyed large tracts of the rain forest. The natural pest predators cannot live without trees, and so many of the conventional growers use chemical insect-killers and if these insect-killers are not used carefully, they can poison other wildlife or wipe out their food chains. Less leaf litter means the soil runs out of nutrients, so artificial fertilizers have to be used. If too much is used, the excess can run off into streams and rivers and pollute them, which harms the animals that live in and depend on the river water.

Konditor & Cook cake and coffee shops can be found around central London neighborhoods. The windows are full of meringues, pastries and cakes – each extremely irresistable. This recipe for Chocolate Biscuit Cake was kindly provided by chef Gerhard Jenne.

KONDITOR & COOK
CHOCOLATE COOKIE CAKE

Preparation time: 15 minutes
Chilling time: 4 hours
Use: 8 x 3-inch loaf pan
Makes: 10 large, very rich slices

$^1/_2$ cup (1 stick) plus 1 tablespoon unsalted butter

$^1/_4$ cup corn syrup

two 3.5-ounce bars dark chocolate, minimum 60% cocoa content, broken into pieces

1 large egg

4 digestive biscuits (cookies) or 2 ounces graham crackers (about 8)

$^1/_2$ cup whole walnuts

$^1/_4$ cup golden raisins

$^1/_3$ cup candied cherries, reserving a few for decoration

Line the loaf pan with parchment paper or alternatively butter the pan. Set aside.

Melt the butter and syrup together in a small saucepan over gentle heat until they begin to boil. Remove from the heat and stir in the chocolate. Continue to stir until melted and smooth. Beat in the egg.

In a separate bowl, break up the cookies or graham crackers into large chunks; remember, they will be broken further when mixed, so don't make them too small. Add the walnuts, raisins and most of the cherries to the broken cookies. Pour the chocolate mixture on to the cookie mixture and mix together with a spatula or wooden spoon.

Press the mixture into the pan and decorate with the reserved cherries. Allow to set in the refrigerator for about 4 hours. Remove from the refrigerator, peel off the paper, and cut into slices or cubes. Serve chilled.

HINT: To make this recipe more child friendly, replace 4 ounces of dark chocolate with milk chocolate.

DARK
ICING

Ideal for covering a sophisticated chocolate cake

one 3.5-ounce bar dark chocolate, minimum 60% cocoa content, chopped

$1/4$ cup ($1/2$ stick) unsalted butter, cubed

Melt the chocolate in a heatproof bowl over a saucepan of simmering water. Remove bowl from the pan, add the butter, and stir until the butter has melted and the sauce has the consistency of thick pouring cream.

Use a small metal spatula to spread the icing over the top and sides of the cake. Let it set. If refrigerated, the icing will lose its sheen.

CHOCOLATE
GLAZE

A traditional, sweet chocolate glaze

one 3.5-ounce bar dark chocolate, minimum 60% cocoa content, chopped

$2/3$ cup confectioners' sugar

3 tablespoons unsalted butter, cubed

3 tablespoons water

Melt the chocolate in a heatproof bowl over a saucepan of simmering water. Sift the confectioners' sugar into the melted chocolate, stir well, then add the butter and stir until incorporated. Remove bowl from the pan and add the water, one tablespoon at a time. Use the glaze while it is still warm – it will run if it is too hot and it will not spread if it is too cold.

DUSKY BUTTER
FROSTING

Ideal for filling and covering a children's cake.

one 3.5-ounce bar milk chocolate

$3/4$ cup ($1 1/2$ sticks) unsalted butter, softened

$1 1/2$ cups confectioners' sugar

Melt the chocolate in a heatproof bowl over a saucepan of simmering water. Remove bowl from pan. Beat the butter and sugar, in a clean bowl. Add the chocolate to the mixture and beat together well.

ORANGE
DUST

A more unusual topping

4 oranges

1¹/₂ cups granulated sugar

¹/₂ cup water

oil for greasing

Scrub the oranges and pat them dry. Using a vegetable peeler, remove the top layer of peel, but ensure you don't remove the white pith. Dissolve the sugar and water in a saucepan then bring to a boil. Continue to boil for about 10 minutes or until it begins to form a heavy syrup – do not allow to caramelize. Add the orange peel and continue to boil without stirring for another 10 minutes. Brush some oil onto a baking sheet and, using a pair of tongs, transfer the caramelized peel to the baking sheet. Let cool and dry completely before pulverizing in a food processor. Store in an airtight container for sprinkling over cakes and puddings.

CHOCOLATE
GANACHE

A thick, rich, and creamy filling or topping. If you need more,
simply increase the quantities, keeping the ingredients in the same proportions.

10 ounces dark chocolate,
minimum 60% cocoa content, finely chopped

1¹/₄ cups heavy cream

Put the chocolate into a large bowl. Heat the cream until it begins to simmer, pour it over the chocolate, and immediately begin to whisk. Continue to whisk until the mixture has cooled and thickened.

NIGELLA'S BLOND
ICING

two 3.5-ounce bars white chocolate

4 tablespoons (¹/₂ stick) unsalted butter

1 cup crème fraîche or sour cream

³/₄ cup confectioners' sugar, sifted

Melt the chocolate and the butter in a heatproof bowl over a saucepan of simmering water. Remove the bowl from the pan. Add the crème fraîche, then gradually beat in the confectioners' sugar. Refrigerate the icing for 10 to 20 minutes so that it sets.

DRINKS TO ACCOMPANY
CHOCOLATE

Micah Carr-Hill is our Product Development Manager and also a serious lover of food. He became interested in wine when he worked in the British wine shop, Oddbins, and eight years later, has poured most of his earnings into buying wine and cooking meals for his friends and his partner, Nat, which can take days to prepare.

Micah believes there should be no rules about what you should and shouldn't drink with particular foods, but says that "chocolate and chocolate desserts are particularly difficult to match as they coat your mouth, are usually quite sweet, and chocolate itself has a certain amount of acidity." He therefore suggests a few tips:

"The one thing to bear in mind when matching wine to desserts is that it is best to choose a wine that is as sweet, if not sweeter, than the food, otherwise the wine is likely to be overpowered by what you are eating and seem unpleasantly sharp.

"However, chocolate does not always go well with traditional sweet wines such as Sauternes, and as chocolate is often married with cherries, raisins, dates, and other such fruits, it often makes sense to match them with drinks that have similar flavors. For example, a chocolate dessert with raspberry would go well with a raspberry liqueur like Framboise or raspberry beer from Belgium.

"Lighter desserts made with white and milk chocolate work well with a fresh, spritzy, grapey Moscato d'Asti or a slightly heavier Orange Muscat (especially if they contain orange). Belgian cherry or raspberry beers would also be good.

"Desserts made with a dark chocolate demand a richer and fuller wine such as a Black Muscat or a sweet Italian Recioto, made from partially dried red wine grapes. You could also try a vin doux naturel, which is a type of French wine that is made from partially fermented wine and local brandy, such as Rivesaltes, Banyuls, or Maury. A port, Ruby or Tawny, an Australian Liqueur Muscat, or even one of the sweeter Madeiras (Malmsey or Bual) would also be good choices.

"If you're serving a savory dish such as a mole, you need a weighty red wine to cope with the range of rich flavors kicking about. A big Syrah, Shiraz, or Zinfandel would cope as would a big Italian red such as an Amarone or Barolo.

"Stouts, porters, and dark beers made from chocolate malts (that have been highly roasted) are also good companions as is black coffee, irrespective of whether there is coffee in the recipe or not.

"The following are my suggestions, but remember that there are no hard and fast rules:

COMPLEMENTARY FLAVORS

APRICOT – light, sweet Muscat or a Hungarian Tokaji

APPLES – sweet Oloroso Sherry or a Liqueur Muscat

BANANA – Australian Liqueur Muscat, Tokaji, sweet Madeira, or Tawny Port

BROWNIES – Black coffee or a good Scotch

COFFEE – Coffee, Orange Muscat, Australian Liqueur Muscat, or a sweet Oloroso sherry such as Matusalem

COOKIES – Tea, coffee, milk

DATES – Liqueur Muscat or sweet Oloroso sherry

FIGS – Black Muscat or sweet Oloroso sherry

GINGER– Ginger beer or ginger ale, sweet Oloroso sherry, or a Liqueur Muscat

GORGONZOLA – Sweet red Italian Recioto, late-bottled vintage Port, or Tawny Port

HARE – a big Syrah, Shiraz, or Zinfandel

HAZELNUTS – a Malmsey or Bual Madeira, or a stout made from chocolate malt

ICE CREAM – a Liqueur Muscat, sweet Oloroso or even a Pedro Ximinez (PX) sherry, a Malmsey, or Bual Madeira

LAMB – a big red from the Rhone Valley, Portugal, or southern Italy

LEMON – a very sweet late-harvest Riesling such as a Trockenbeerenauslese

MEXICAN – Chilean or Argentinian red wine, Mexican beer, or a cocktail such as a Margarita or Bloody Mary

PANNA COTTA – Recioto di Soave from Italy or an Orange Muscat

PEARS – Orange Muscat

PECAN PIE – Liqueur Muscat, sweet Oloroso Muscat, or a Malmsey or Bual Madeira

STOUT CAKE – stout

TRUFFLES – eau de vie of your choice

VANILLA – late-harvest Riesling

VENISON – big Italian red such as a Barolo or something from the south of Italy such as a Salice Salentino

WALNUTS – Australian Liqueur Muscat or a sweet Oloroso sherry

WHITE CHOCOLATE sweet white Bordeaux such as Sauternes or Barsac, or a late-harvest Riesling such as an Auslese or Beerenauslese".

Lubaantun was the center of the Maya civilization in southern Belize. A great ceremonial focus, it existed over 1,000 years ago, hidden deep in the rain forest.

In this vibrant society, the universal measure of value was the cocoa bean. As Lubaantun was situated in the Maya mountains, where cacao trees thrived in the wild, it rapidly became the economic center of the Maya world, with the cocoa bean at the heart of the economy.

In the 1850s, it was taken over by colonists, who cut down trees and established plantations. But they struggled to control nature and place names like "Go To Hell Creek" and "Hellgate" are all that remains of those desperate times.

The Maya returned to their villages in the mountains and lived by subsistence farming, trading their surplus cocoa beans for cash and growing indigenous crops using traditional methods. But in the early 1990s the price of cocoa, which had been falling for years, dropped dramatically just before harvest time as too much cocoa flooded world markets and many farmers were left unable to afford even to harvest their crops.

It was at this time that Jo Fairley and Craig Sams, who were on vacation in Belize and looking for organic cocoa beans, heard about their plight. They began to buy organic beans from the Maya, which in turn, led to their involvement with the Fairtrade foundation. Their relationship with the Toledo Cocoa Growers Association resulted in the creation of Green & Black's

Maya Gold Chocolate, sold in the UK, and the first-ever product to carry the Fairtrade Mark.

Over 300 families benefit from the sale of cocoa beans and many of the farmers have plantations with trees that are over 100 years old. They live on the land that their ancestors have farmed for thousands of years and will preserve that land for future generations.

OLD TIMERS

Saul Garcia is a Fairtrade farmer who has been farming cacao in Belize for thirty-eight years. If you visit his fifteen-acre farm set on the banks of the Columbia River, you can see more than fifteen different varieties of cacao tree, surrounded by a cascade of beautiful colors from the shrubs and crops that he plants between his cacao trees.

The bio-diversity created by planting so many different species of cacao and other plants helps to reduce the threat of bugs that cause serious damage to organically grown cacao.

Papaya, bananas, coffee, breebee, coconut, mango, breadfruit, cacao, mamey sapote, lime, *Theobroma bicolor*, avocado, cohune palm, soursop, plantain, samwood, jippy japa, golden plum, leucaena, glyricidia, craboo, orange, starfruit, vanilla, ginger, sugar cane, sorrel, and bamboo are just some of the plants Saul Garcia grows. Some are used for food or as fiber, particularly for basket weaving, others are good for the soil and there are also ornamental plants for attracting pollinators.

INDEX

INDEX

ACKNOWLEDGEMENTS

Green & Black's and Caroline Jeremy would like to thank all the staff, past and present, at Green & Black's especially Micah Carr-Hill, Cluny Brown, and Mark Palmer; all the farmers who grow cacao for us; Jo Fairley and Craig Sams, our founders; all those people whose recipes have been included in this book; Christopher Nesbitt who has been the driving force behind the development of the T.C.G.A. in Belize, and his wife Dawn; Claire Fry who designed the book; Francesca Yorke for her photographs; David Morgan, the home economist; Wei Tang for her prop styling; the recipe testers Jo Gilks, Sally Leighton, Gilly Booth, and Sofia Craxton; Kyle Cathie, Muna Reyal, and Ana Sampson at Kyle Cathie, our publishers; Pearlfisher, our packaging design company; Phipps PR; and Delora Jones and Susie Theodorou for adapting and developing the American edition.

We would also like to thank the following chefs, authors, and publishers for giving us permission to use their recipes:

Alastair Little and Richard Whittington, Fudge Sauce, *Keep It Simple* (Conran Octopus 1993)
Tavola, 155 Westbourne Grove, London W11 2RS, England

Dodi Miller, Mole Poblano de Guajolote, Cool Chile Co., P.O. Box 5702, London W11 2GS, England

Elisabeth Luard, Italian Venison Agridolce, more recipes in *Latin American Kitchen* (Kyle Books 2004)

Elizabeth Weisberg and Rachel Duffield,
Lighthouse Bakery Chocolate Bread, Lighthouse Bakery, 64 Northcote Road, London SW11 6QL, England

Gerard Coleman and Anne Weyns, Chocolate and Salted Caramel Tart,
L'Artisan du Chocolat, 89 Lower Sloane Street, London SW1 8DA, England

Gerhard Jenne, Chocolate Cookie Cake, Konditor & Cook, 22 Cornwall Road, London SE1 8TW, England

Launceston Place, Chocolate Berry Torte, Launceston Place 1a, Launceston Place, London W8, England

Lorna Wing, Sachertorte, Lorna Wing Ltd., 48 Westover Road, London SW18 2RH, England

Clementine Cake from *How to Eat* by Nigella Lawson, published by Chatto & Windus. Reprinted by permission of The Random House Group Ltd.

Nora Carey, Chestnut and Chocolate Soufflés,
Perfect Preserves Provisions from the Kitchen Garden (Stewart, Tabori & Chang, 1990)

Paul and Jeanne Rankin, White Chocolate and Hazelnut Cheesecake, *Hot Chefs* (BBC Worldwide, 1992)
www.cayennerestaurant.com

Rachel Green, Chocolate and Lemongrass Mousse,
Rachel Green's Food Design, The Barn, St. Leonard's Lane, South Cockerington, Louth, Lincolnshire LN11 7EF, England

Sue Lawrence, Chocolate Crusted Lemon Tart, *Book of Baking* (Headline 2004)

Valentina Harris, Tuscan Sweet and Sour Hare, *Regional Italian Cooking* (BBC Worldwide)
www.villavalentina.com (Cooking school in Tuscany).

White Chocolate Cardamom Mousse Reprinted by kind permission of Harper Collins Publishers Ltd.
© Nigel Slater, *Real Food* (1999)

Whole Earth Foods, Cocoa Crunch, Kallo Foods, Wormley, Surrey GU8 5SZ, England

We also thank the following organizations:
The Fairtrade Foundation, Suite 204, 16 Baldwin's Gardens, London EC1N 7RJ Tel: 44 20 7405 5942 www.fairtrade.org.uk
Soil Association, Bristol House, 40–56 Victoria Street, Bristol BS1 6BY Tel: 44 117 929 0661 www.soilassociation.org
Toledo Cacao Growers Association, Punta Gorda Depot, Main Road, Punta Gorda, Toledo District, Belize.

Caroline would also like to thank her husband, David, and children Oscar, Edward, Chloë, and Oliver for their tasting skills, patience and enthusiasm for all things chocolate; Claire Fry, Jo Gilks, Gilly Booth, Beverley Patrick, and Sally Johnston for endless creative thought, animated discussion, and laughter.

This edition published in 2007 by Kyle Books,
an imprint of Kyle Cathie Limited.
general.enquiries@kyle-cathie.com
www.kylecathie.com

First published in 2004

Distributed by National Book Network
4501 Forbes Blvd., Suite 200
Lanham, MD 20706
Phone: (301) 459 3366
Fax: (301) 429 5746

ISBN 978-1-904920-670
10 9 8 7 6 5 4 3 2

Compiled by Caroline Jeremy
Senior Editor Muna Reyal
Designer Claire Fry
Photographer Francesca Yorke
American Food Editor Susie Theodorou
Text Americanizer Delora Jones
Home economist David Morgan
Copy editor Stephanie Horner
Recipe testing Jo Gilks, Sally Leighton, Gilly Booth
Styling Wei Tang
Production Sha Huxtable

The Library of Congress Cataloguing-in-Publication Data is available on file.

Color reproduction by Colourscan
Printed and bound in Singapore by Tien-Wah Press